Soccer Training Blueprints

15 Ready-to-Run Sessions for Outstanding Attacking Play

James Jordan

Oakamoor Publishing

Published in 2016 by Oakamoor Publishing, an imprint of Bennion Kearny Limited.

Copyright © Oakamoor Publishing

ISBN: 978-1-910773-32-1

All Rights Reserved. No part of this publication may be reproduced, stored in a retrieval system, or transmitted in any form or by any means, electronic, mechanical, photocopying, recording or otherwise, without the prior permission of the publisher.

This book is sold subject to the condition that it shall not, by way of trade or otherwise, be lent, re-sold, hired out or otherwise circulated without the publisher's prior consent in any form of binding or cover other than that it which it is published and without a similar condition including this condition being imposed on the subsequent purchaser.

Bennion Kearny has endeavoured to provide trademark information about all the companies and products mentioned in this book by the appropriate use of capitals. However, Bennion Kearny cannot guarantee the accuracy of this information.

Published by Oakamoor Publishing, Bennion Kearny Limited
6 Woodside
Churnet View Road
Oakamoor
Staffordshire
ST10 3AE

Cover image: Licensed from alongzo/Shutterstock.com

About the Author

James Jordan is an educator and a soccer coach. He holds the NSCAA Premier Diploma, USSF National Youth License, and a Doctorate in Education. Using Game-based Soccer techniques developed over the past decade, his teams (boys and girls) have won six high school state championships and one Classic 1 boys' club championship.

James blogs at: www.jamesedwardjordan.com

Table of Contents

What is Game-based Soccer? | 1
How Will This Book Help Your Players Create and Score More Goals? | 2

Session #1: Dribbling to Keep Possession | 4
Warm-up Activity: Tag | 5
Activity #1: Introduction to The Gate Dribbling Game | 6
Activity #2: The Gate Dribbling Game with Pressure | 7
Activity #3: Unbalanced Possession | 8
End of Practice Scrimmage: Half Field Scrimmage with Gates | 9

Session #2: The Importance of First Touch | 11
Warm-up Activity: Soccer Pong | 12
Activity #1: The Circle Game | 14
Activity #2: The Circle Game With Pressure | 15
Activity #3: 6v6 Plus 6 | 16
End of Practice Scrimmage: First Touch Boxes | 17

Session #3: Pass and Move to Create Space | 19
Warm-up Activity: The Gate Passing Game | 20
Activity #1: 4v1 | 22
Activity #2: Basic Possession | 23
Activity #3: 2v1 Continuous*Wide | 24

End of Practice Scrimmage: 2/3 Field Scrimmage | 25

Session #4: Exploding Past Defenders | 27
Warm-up Activity: Sharks and Minnows | 28
Activity #1: 1v1 Grid | 29
Activity #2: The End Zone Game | 30
Activity #3: 1v1 to Goal with Goalkeepers | 31
End of Practice Scrimmage: Beat the Defender | 33

Session #5: Finishing in the Box | 34
Warm-up Activity: World Cup | 35
Activity #1: The Penalty Box Shooting Game | 36
Activity #2: Outside In | 38
Activity #3: 2v1 Continuous*Stacked | 39
End of Practice Scrimmage: Two Touch Inside the Box | 40

Session #6: The Give and Go | 42
Warm-up Activity: Soccer Pong | 43
Activity #1: The Gate Passing Game | 44
Activity #2: The Nickens | 46
Activity #3: 2v1 Continuous*Side by Side | 47
End of Practice Scrimmage: Beat the Offside Line | 49

Session #7: Introduction to Scoring Goals in Transition | 50
Warm-up Activity: The Nickens in Transition | 51
Activity #1: Target Ball in Transition | 53
Activity #2: 2v1 Continuous*Side by Side | 54
Activity #3: 3v2 Continuous*Stacked and Wide | 55
End of Practice Scrimmage: Half Field Transition | 57

Session #8: Scoring with the Laces | 58
Warm-up Activity: The Circle Game | 59
Activity #1: The Penalty Box Shooting Game | 60
Activity #2: 6v6 Plus 6 | 61
Activity #3: 2v1 Continuous*Stacked | 62
End of Practice Scrimmage: Half Field Scrimmage | 64

Session #9: Creating Opportunities from Wide Areas | 66
Warm-up Activity: Headers and Volleys | 67
Activity #1: Introduction to the Crossing Game | 68
Activity #2: 2v1 Continuous*Ball Starts Wide | 70
Activity #3: 3v2 Continuous*Ball Starts Wide | 71
End of Practice Scrimmage: Get it to the Wingers! | 72

Session #10: The Overlap | 74
Warm-up Activity: The Circle Game | 75
Activity #1: The Nickens Plus One | 76
Activity #2: 2v1 Continuous*Overlap | 77
Activity #3: 3v2 Continuous*Overlap | 79
End of Practice Scrimmage: Half Field Scrimmage | 80

Session #11: Short, Short Long | 81
Warm-up Activity: 5v2 | 82
Activity #1: Over the River | 84
Activity #2: End Zone Game with a Target | 85
Activity #3: 3v2 Continuous*Stacked and Level | 86
End of Practice Scrimmage: Half Field Scrimmage with Bumpers | 88

Session #12: Switching the Point of the Attack | 89
Warm-up Activity: The Circle Game With Pressure | 90
Activity #1: Target Ball | 91
Activity #2: The 6 Small Goal Game | 93
Activity #3: 3v2 Continuous*Stacked and Wide* Ball Starts Wide | 94
End of Practice Scrimmage: Full Field Scrimmage | 95

Session #13: Introduction to Converting from Crosses | 97
Warm-up Activity: Flying Wingers | 98
Activity #1: The Crossing Game*Progression #1 | 99
Activity #2: The Crossing Game*Progression #2 | 100
Activity #3: 2v1 Continuous*Wide*Ball Passed in | 101
End of Practice Scrimmage: 18s Extended Out | 103

Session #14: Introduction to Using a Target Player | 104
Warm-up Activity: The Circle Game With Defensive Pressure | 105
Activity #1: End Zone Game with a Target Under Pressure | 106
Activity #2: 6v6 Plus 2 Targets | 107
Activity #3: 3v2 Continuous*Double Stacked | 108
End of Practice Scrimmage: Hit the Targets! | 109

Session #15: Introduction to Getting Numbers in the Attack | 111
Warm-up Activity: 5v2*Outside | 112
Activity #1: End Zone Game with Targets and Goals | 113
Activity #2: The 2 Zone Game | 114
Activity #3: The 3 Zone Game | 116
End of Practice Scrimmage: Get Over the Halfway Line! | 117

The Final Whistle | 119

What is Game-based Soccer?

This book is composed of 15 session plans, all of which are based on the concept of Game-based Soccer.

Game-based soccer training is the philosophy that all practice activities can, and should, be turned into a game. By "game", I mean that there are winners and losers. The players can compete against themselves, each other, in teams, or all together against a target.

There should always be consequences for the losing person/team in this approach. It does not have to be a big consequence, nor should it have to be a physical consequence, but the players should develop a mindset in which it pays to win. Consequences should depend on the activity/game, as well as the age group, but they can range from resetting the balls for the next game, to the winning team getting their water first, to 10 sit-ups to a short sprinting exercise. The goal is not to punish players and discourage them from thinking of physical activity as a negative, but it should be just enough to motivate the players to try harder to win next time!

A Game-based Soccer approach recognizes that soccer is a dynamic game, where the variables are many and the stoppages are few. In order to be successful, players need to understand and be able to play in all positions on the field. As this particular book focuses on developing attacking players, attacking concepts will be emphasized.

In essence, Game-based Soccer encourages coaches to create an environment in which every player is incentivized to compete at his or her highest level. This is where the biggest developmental gains are made, both individually and collectively. How do you set up an environment where players are always incentivized to give their best? Make everything a competition with consequences for the losers.

As the coach, it is up to you to determine the most productive ways to define competition for your team; for example, some games are more suited to competition against an external target, a player competing against his previous best score, or two individuals/teams facing off against each other. The goal is to make the consequence just enough to incentivize the losing player/team to try harder next time and also to encourage the winning team to up their game so that they don't have to do the consequence. Obviously, with younger players, you don't want the consequence to be seen as a "punishment" and to destroy their love for the game. If in any doubt, allow the "winning team" to get water first, while the "losing team" resets the balls/picks up the cones, etc.

How Will This Book Help Your Players Create and Score More Goals?

Creating and scoring goals is something that all coaches of all teams strive to accomplish. If you implement the session plans in this book, your players will create and score more goals for the following reasons:

- **Each session has a single focus**
  Often, we, as coaches, get caught up in trying to coach everything. This frequently leads to confusion and detracts from what we are trying to accomplish. Thus, every activity for every session in this book directly relates to the topic/focus for the day.
- **Each session's activities follow a logical and efficient progression**
  This way, you are not wasting time setting up new grids. In many cases, you can simply repurpose the old grid by moving a few cones and/or adding goals. Additionally, each session moves from simple activities to more complex ones, so players find success early and the learning process is accelerated.
- **Each activity includes progressions**
  This allows you to repeat aspects, or a complete session multiple times throughout the season without having to do the exact same session. Your players will already know the basic setup and so you can move more quickly through the progressions. Some groups will love some activities/progressions and you will be able to use that activity as a vehicle to accomplish different goals throughout the season. For example, one season, I had a group that just loved Target Ball, so I used it many times to teach different concepts.
- **Each session is centred on the Game-based Soccer philosophy**
  Utilizing a Game-based Soccer approach will help you to create a culture of competition in your team; it will increase your players' speed of play; your players' technique will be learned, tested, and improved under game-like conditions; your players will be exposed to more learning situations; and your practices will be a lot of fun because there will be no (or minimal) lines, lectures or laps!
- **Each session comes with Guided Discovery Questions**
  As a corollary to the Game-based Soccer approach, Guided Discovery is a method that is becoming increasingly popular amongst coaches as they recognize that the best way to empower their players is to make them students of the game and to ask them questions. This is also known as the Socratic

Method and is similar to the facilitator/guide-on-the-side approach that is replacing the traditional direct instruction/lecture method in classrooms.

Session #1: Dribbling to Keep Possession

This session is designed to introduce your players to the role of the first attacker when confronted by a defender(s) and maintaining possession of the ball is the primary goal. It is appropriate for any level of player and can also be used at the beginning of the season to make sure all players know the basics of escaping pressure when necessary.

What will players learn from this session?

- These activities force players to confront a 1v1 battle. The aim is to escape pressure and keep possession of the ball (attacking mindset and ball control).
- Players constantly change pace and direction with the ball in a confined space (mobility).
- Successful players, especially the ones who are not the fastest, will start to disguise their movements (improvisation).
- Successful players keep their head up and eyes open to see where the space is, but also to recognize the visual cues of the defender (e.g., where is she looking, are they favoring one particular side, are they weak on one side, what is their body position?).

Coaching Points for the session:
Praise players when they "take a look" to see where the space is.

- Praise players when they are able to escape pressure with their first touch.
- Praise players when they are able to escape pressure with a turn.
- Praise players when they are able to escape pressure with some kind of "move".
- Praise creativity (even when it doesn't come off).
- Praise players when they disguise their intentions.
- Praise players who change speed and direction to escape pressure.

Guided discovery questions for the session: (can be asked at any point)

- Is it easier or harder to escape pressure when you go fast or slow? Why?
- Is it easier or harder to escape pressure when you change pace and direction? Why?
- What kind of moves can you use to be successful in escaping pressure? What do you think makes them work?

- How can you read the defender's body language and positioning to know what to do?

Warm-up Activity: Tag

Time: Approximately 10 minutes.

Area: Approximately 15 x 15 yards (L x W) - the grid's size depends on your numbers (how big/small you want to make it). Remember, making it bigger will make it easier for the dribblers. If you have large numbers, consider making two (or more) grids (and splitting by ability).

Activity: All players apart from the tagger(s) start with a ball and their task is to stay inside the grid and not get tagged by the tagger(s). Select a tagger or pair of taggers. Once a dribbler gets tagged, she must do 25 toe taps (or some other stationary skill that you want repeating), then stand with a foot on the ball and one hand in the air. She is then eligible to be "high-fived" back into the game by a dribbler. The objective for the taggers is to have all the dribblers standing with their hands in the air. Play the game as many times as is necessary to allow all the kids their turn at being a tagger (stop games that go on for longer than 30-45 seconds - or join in and help!). Give the tagger(s) a pinnie/bib!

Possible Progressions:

- Change the number of toe taps/insides players have to do.
- Instead of toe taps, have players do a certain number of ball juggles (e.g., 10 "feet only").
- Mandate that players can only use a certain foot (e.g., only left foot or only right foot) in the grid.
- Add a tagger(s); make the grid bigger/smaller.

Activity #1: Introduction to The Gate Dribbling Game

Time: Approximately 15 minutes.

Area: 25 x 25 yards (L x W) or larger depending on how many players you have.

Activity: Put players in pairs with a ball. Set up a number of 1.5-yard-wide gates randomly arranged in your grid. The size and number of gates can vary depending on the number of players you have and their skill level. I would start with at least as many gates as players. If you have a large group, create two grids, or have one group working while the other group rests. Players score a point for each gate they dribble the ball through. Go for 30-45 seconds and have each player keep count of how many points they score. See how many they get and ask how the top-scoring player got so many. Get them to do a quick demonstration. Repeat and see if players beat their original score. If your players are struggling with this game, make the gates bigger and/or change their locations. The objective is simply to get them dribbling in different directions with the ball under control. You should always start an activity by making it as simple as possible, so that players can quickly find success. Once they understand the game, that's when you can start to make it progressively more challenging.

Possible Progressions:

- Add a restriction whereby players can only dribble with their left foot (or right foot).
- Add a restriction whereby players can only go through a gate using a certain surface (e.g., toe, laces, sole, etc.).
- Replace some of the gates with pinnies (or different colored cones) and say that players must go through a cone gate followed by a pinnie gate (or different colored cone gate).
- Make the gates smaller and/or reduce the number of gates.

Activity #2: The Gate Dribbling Game with Pressure

Time: Approximately 15 minutes.

Area: 25 x 25 yards (L x W) or larger depending on how many players you have.

Activity: This activity is a progression from the previous one, which will allow you to give your players a quick water break and then get straight back into action. This time, start with a "bandit" whose job is to stop players from dribbling through the gates. Change the bandit every 30-45 seconds (get them to keep score of how many balls they kicked away).

Possible Progressions:

- Add a restriction whereby players can only dribble with their left foot (or right foot).
- Add another bandit (2 bandits at a time).
- Replace some of the gates with pinnies (or different colored cones) and say that players must go through a cone gate followed by a pinnie gate (or different colored cone gate).
- Add another bandit (3 bandits at a time).
- Make the gates smaller and/or reduce the number of gates.
- Add another bandit (4 bandits at a time).

Activity #3: Unbalanced Possession

Time: Approximately 15 minutes

Area: 50 x 60 yards (W x L), or as close to half a game field as you can get. Start big, you can always make it smaller.

Activity: Split players up into two teams. One team should have a clear advantage in numbers (e.g. 8v4, 10v5, etc.), with that team's objective being to keep the ball for as long as possible (a coach can keep count by counting the seconds out loud – I would suggest the first 5 are in your head!). Give players a certain amount of time (e.g., 3 minutes) and then take the highest number of consecutive seconds in possession from each team to declare a winner. Keep rotating the players, so they are not always on the chasing/possession team. If you have a large number of players (e.g., more than 20), you may want to consider using 2 smaller grids (in order to maximize the players' number of touches and learning situations). If you have fewer players (e.g., 12 or less), you may want to make the field smaller.

Possible Progressions:

- Make it so teams score a goal by keeping the ball for 10 seconds. Play first team to score 3 goals, wins.
- Put the possession team on a touch restriction (e.g., 3 touch maximum, 2 touch maximum).
- Add a halfway line and mandate that teams may only starting counting seconds in possession when the ball is in the opponents' half.

End of Practice Scrimmage:
Half Field Scrimmage with Gates

Time: Approximately 30 minutes (or whatever is left of practice).

Area: One half of the field. Add a gate (width of approximately 5 yards) on the halfway line on each flank (see diagram). By putting a Coerver goal on the halfway line, you can have two of these scrimmages at the same time. Depending on your numbers, you may want to play the entire width of the field or just the width of the 18-yard box. Typically, I will play the width of the 18 for 5v5 - 7v7; however, if you find that space too restrictive, you can always open it up.

Activity: Goals are scored in the usual way in the two big goals, but also by dribbling through one of the gates on either flank. This will encourage players to dribble the ball and look for the "open" gate, as well as the regular goal. Play even numbers and arrange teams in a formation that reflects your desired game day formation. For example, if you are playing 8v8, you can put teams in a 3-3-1 formation (this gives you central players as well as wide players on both defense and offense). Alternately, you can set up one (or both) of the teams in a 2-3-2 formation to change things up. This is a good game to play if you have the space and the numbers. If you don't, no need to worry, just divide up the players into two even teams and let them play in the space you have available.

Progressions:
- Add a gate in the middle of the field.
- Have fixed goalkeepers, but play transition, so when one team scores in one goal, they immediately get the ball back and now go to the other goal (other team switches, too).
- Take away the goalkeepers (will encourage players to take offensive risks).
- Add a neutral(s) to give the team in possession an advantage.
- Put one or both teams on touch restrictions (e.g., 3 touch max, 2 touch max, 1 touch max!).

Session #2: The Importance of First Touch

This session is designed to introduce your players to the importance of first touch. It can be modified for any age group and/or ability levels because this concept is critical to every player's success. The warm-up and first two activities will give your players lots of touches on the ball, building in context from simple and isolated to more game-like. The third activity is a game that emphasizes a first touch to set up a goal-scoring opportunity.

What will players learn from this session?
- Players learn to integrate a change of pace and direction with movement away and to the ball, while figuring out the most appropriate surface of the foot, angle of the body, and with which foot they should control the ball to set themselves up for success (mobility, support, attacking mindset, and technique).
- Players receive the ball under pressure and must make a decision about how to keep it away from predators in a confined space (improvisation).
- Players learn to recognize the visual cues as players "check" to receive the ball. Ultimately, they start to look for the "tells" that someone wants the ball, and where they should play it (attacking mindset).
- Successful players keep their head up and eyes open to see where the space is, but also to recognize the visual cues of the defender(s) (e.g., where is she looking, are they favoring one particular side, are they weak on one side, what is their body position?).

Coaching Points for the session:
- Praise players when they change speed and direction to check for the ball.
- Praise players when they try to take their first touch away from pressure.
- Praise players when they experiment by using different surfaces of the feet to control the ball.
- Praise players when they try to control a ball on the move.
- Praise players when they take a look at the "picture" (where people are/space is on the field) before they control the ball.
- Praise players when they take a first touch that sets them up for the next action (shot, pass, dribble, etc.).

Guided discovery questions for the session: (can be asked at any point)

- What surface of your foot is it easiest to control the ball with? Why?
- What is the best way to control the ball on the run? Why do you think this is?
- What angle can you come to the ball at, in order to turn and pass more easily?
- What can people on the inside/outside of the circle communicate to make this activity more successful?
- Why is it important to change pace when checking for the ball?
- Why is it important for people on the outside to be on their toes and constantly surveying?
- How can you read the defender's body language and positioning to know what to do?

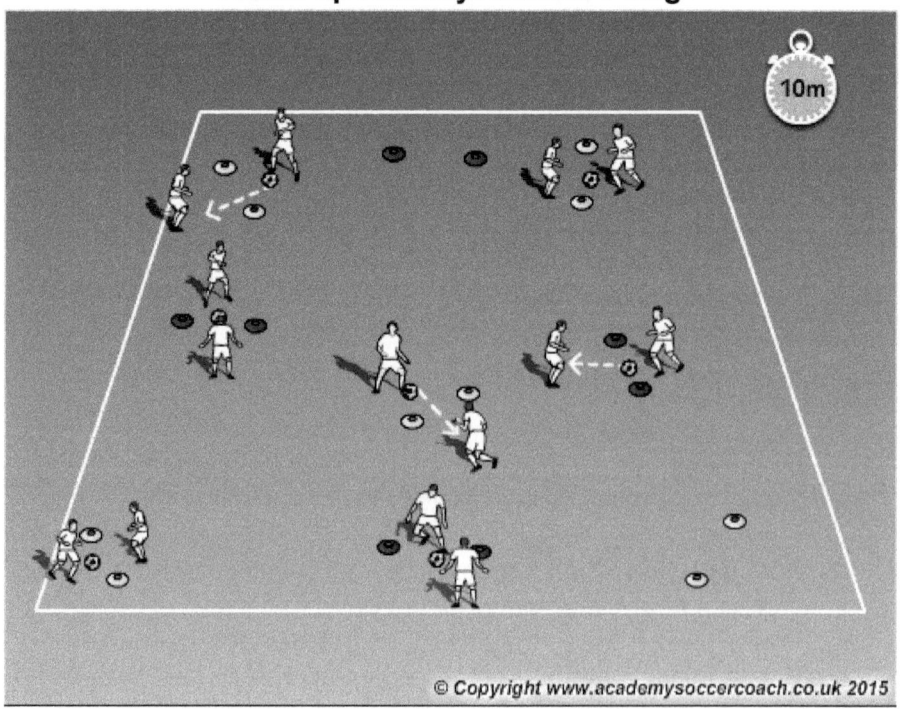

Warm-up Activity: Soccer Pong

Time: Approximately 10 minutes

Area: Big open space

Activity: Two players play against each other and share a ball. They place two cones anywhere from 2-5 yards apart. Players pass back and forth to each other. The rules are that the ball must never stop, must always stay on the ground and must go through the two cones without touching them. Whenever this is violated the other person receives a point. Because of the rule that the ball must never stop, players have to play 1-2 touch. The closer the two cones are, the closer the pairs are probably going to be. The farther apart they are, the more they will have to move laterally and look more like the old arcade game "Pong". Play for a specified amount of time (e.g., 60 seconds) and see which pair can become the champions. If your players are struggling with this game, make the gates bigger and/or mandate that each player takes two touches (this will slow the game down some, but will reduce the number of mistakes as players attempt to be too aggressive). The objective is simply to get them passing with their partner and working on their first touch.

Possible Progressions:

- Make a "ladder" and, after each game, have players move up and down if they win/lose.
- Impose a maximum touch limitation (e.g., 2 touches, or 1 touch).
- Change the width of the gates.

*The higher the level of your team's players, the sooner they will figure out how to "game the system" by standing closer to the gate and hitting the ball as hard as they can. If you find this happening, you can make it a cooperative game by having the players count the number of passes they can achieve back and forth through the gate. This happened to me. By modifying the game, we were still able to get lots of passes back and forth through the gate. I also started mandating the number of touches and how far away they were from the gate to vary the game.

Activity #1: The Circle Game

Time: Approximately 20 minutes.

Area: Put players in a circle with a radius of 10-12 yards. An easy way to do this is to put down a cone and then walk out 10-12 yards at 4 points and tell the players to make a circle around the 4 "point" cones.

Activity: Have the players get in a circle (ideally around the centre circle; if there is not one available, create your own). There should be equal spacing between each player. For organizational purposes, create 2 groups. Number each player 1 or 2 (should be an equal number of each). Have the group of 1s come to the middle of the circle; the 2s are on the outside. The 2s should have a ball at their feet. Once the game gets going, there are simply players in the middle receiving and passing and players on the outside who are passing and receiving. Working in intervals of 30-45 seconds, the outside players pass the ball to players in the middle whose job it is play it right back to the passer first time. Have the inside players keep count of their completed passes. The person with the fewest passes performs a quick (5 second) consequence (e.g., 20 toe taps) on the outside of the circle. In order to improve technique, players need repetitions. In this activity, players work under increasingly game-like conditions as pressure and difficulty intensify. Ensure that they are checking for the ball at speed to begin with (later on, if they don't, they will never get the ball!).

Possible Progressions:

- Mandate the players on the inside to use a certain foot (e.g., only right, then only left, then either foot).
- Every player must take two touches (mandate a certain surface to control the ball; e.g., only the outside of the foot, only the inside, only the sole, etc.).
- Take away a ball (creates competition in the middle for a ball; leads to receiving under pressure).
- Take away another ball (intensifies the above).
- Have outside players serve the ball from their hands in the air (e.g., knee height, chest height, bouncing ball).

Activity #2: The Circle Game With Pressure

Time: Approximately 20 minutes.

Activity: This activity is a progression from the previous one, which will allow you to give your players a quick water break and then get straight back into action. This time, create 3 groups. Number each player 1, 2, or 3. Have the group of 1s come to the middle of the circle; the 2s and 3s are on the outside. The 2s should have a ball at their feet, while the 3s should be "open". This situation (where the 2s have the balls and the 3s don't) is only to get the activity started. Once the game gets going, there are simply players in the middle receiving and passing and players on the outside who are passing and receiving. Working in intervals of 30-45 seconds, the outside players pass the ball to players in the middle whose job is to pass it back to a different person. Have the inside players keep count of their completed passes. The person with the fewest passes does a quick consequence (e.g. 20 tic tocs, 20 toe taps, etc.) on the outside of the circle.

Possible Progressions:

- Mandate the players on the inside to use a certain foot (e.g., only right, then only left, then either foot).
- Every player must take two touches (mandate a certain surface to control the ball; e.g., only the outside of the foot, only the inside, only the sole, etc.).
- Take away a ball (creates competition in the middle for a ball; leads to receiving under pressure).
- Take away another ball (intensifies the above).
- Have outside players serve the ball from their hands in the air (e.g., knee height, chest height, bouncing ball).

Activity #3: 6v6 Plus 6

Time: Approximately 20 minutes.

Area: If you have a marked 18-yard box, use it and then mark out another one with cones to create a 36 x 44 yards (L x W) playing grid.

Activity: This game works best with 20 players (2 goalkeepers and 18 outfield players), but can easily be modified to fit your numbers. Divide the players into 3 even (ability) teams with a goalkeeper in each goal. The balls should be divided evenly and placed in each goal for quick and easy retrieval by the goalkeeper. The players on the team that is "out", position themselves around the edge of the field (1 on each long side, and 1 either side of each goal). These players serve as "bumpers," have 1 touch, and play on whichever team passes them the ball – in essence, they are neutrals. There are no offsides in this game. Play first team to a set number of goals (e.g., 2, 3) and give the losing team a consequence. The losing team then switches with the "bumper" team.

Possible Progressions:

- Give 2 points for each goal that comes directly from a "bumper" player.
- Put all players inside the grid on a touch restriction (e.g., 2 touch maximum).
- Mandate that all goals must be a first time finish.

End of Practice Scrimmage: First Touch Boxes

Time: Approximately 30 minutes (or whatever is left of practice).

Area: One half of the field. In each of the corners, make a 4x4 yard box in which a player will stand (there will be four boxes and two players from each team will occupy boxes). By putting a Coerver goal on the halfway line, you can have two of these scrimmages at the same time. Depending on your numbers, you may want to play the entire width of the field or just the width of the 18-yard box. Typically, I will play the width of the 18 for 5v5 - 7v7; however, if you find that space too restrictive, you can always open it up.

Activity: Goals are scored by passing to a teammate in a box. If the player receiving the ball can control the ball without it leaving the box (testing the first touch), his team gets a point. Defenders are not allowed in the boxes. When a team scores a point, the player who passed the ball into the box switches with the player who just received it. This ensures that players aren't standing in boxes for long periods of time.

Progressions:

- Make the boxes bigger or smaller, depending on the skill levels of your players.
- Allow the defending team into the boxes.
- Make additional boxes in the middle of the field and/or on the flanks.
- Put one or both teams on touch restrictions (e.g., 3 touch max, 2 touch max, 1 touch max!).
- Remove the boxes and play with the regular goals.

Session #3: Pass and Move to Create Space

This session is designed to introduce your players to the fundamental attacking concept of passing and moving to create space. Again, this session is appropriate for any level of player and can also be used at the beginning of the season to make sure all players know the basics of passing the ball and how they fit into a team that tries to keep possession of the ball.

What will players learn from this session?

- [The first activity] demands players to work together as they look for open gates to pass through (support).
- This session encourages players to develop spatial awareness and move accordingly in order to help their team to maintain possession of the ball (support, mobility, width, depth).
- This session also develops close ball control, use of both feet, and encourages sharp changes of pace and direction in a relatively crowded area (mobility and improvisation).
- Successful players will keep their head up and eyes open to see where the space is, but also to recognize the visual cues of the defender (e.g., where is she looking, are they favoring one particular side, are they weak on one side, what is their body position?).
- Players must solve the problem of escaping pressure in a confined space (improvisation).
- This session encourages players to switch the point of the attack to a less well-defended area and to play in tight spaces where necessary (width and improvisation).

Coaching Points for the session:
Praise players when they "take a look" to see where the space is.

- Praise creativity (even when it doesn't come off).
- Praise players for trying to keep possession of the ball and not panicking (booting the ball).
- Praise players who make intelligent angles for the ball (try to stay away from square angles).
- Praise players who make good angles but don't receive the ball (they are most likely creating space for someone else).
- Praise players who make good pass selection decisions (not necessarily execution).

Guided discovery questions for the session: (can be asked at any point)

- What surfaces of the foot are the most useful here? Why do you think this is?

- [In the first activity] What do partners need to do to be successful at this game? Show me.
- [In the first activity] How do you know where the open gates are? Show me.
- [In the first activity] What is the best distance between partners so that you can be most efficient? Show me.
- What can you do to support your teammate when she has the ball? Show me.
- What types of things can you communicate to make it easier for your teammate(s)?
- Should we be making the field as big as possible or group together? Why?
- Should you be aiming to play fast or slow? Why?
- Where should you aim to take your first touch to avoid the defenders taking the ball? How?
- Is it easier to keep the ball when it is on the ground or in the air? Why?
- Do you always want to play short passes in this game? Why?
- What are the visual cues to send a long ball, as opposed to a short pass? Explain that to me.
- Why is the weak side so important in this game? Explain that to me.

Warm-up Activity: The Gate Passing Game

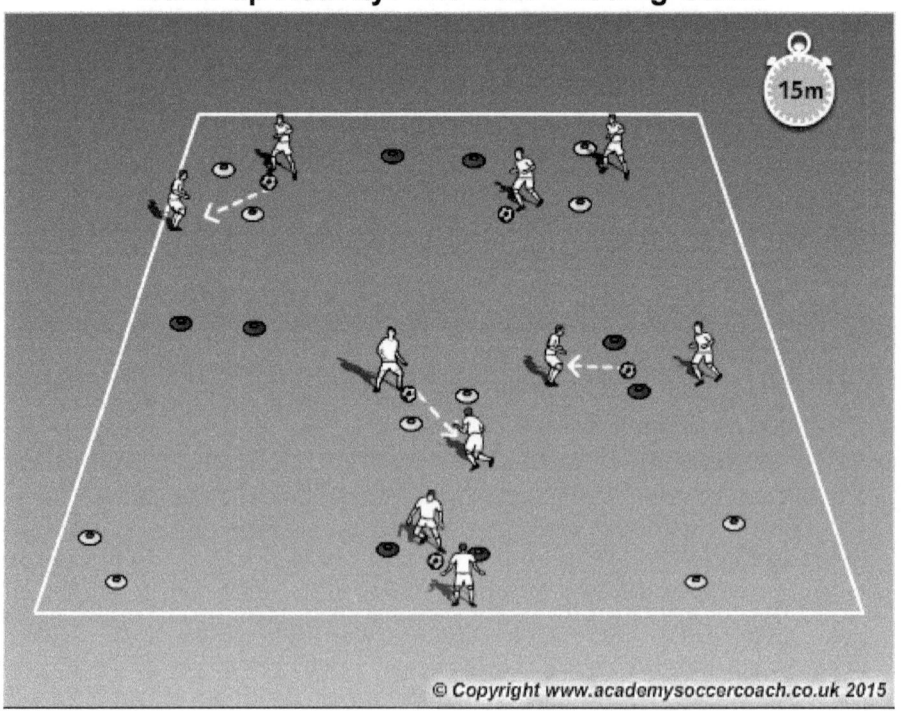

Time: Approximately 15 minutes.

Area: 25x25 yards (L x W) or larger, depending on how many players you have.

Activity: Put players in pairs with a ball. Set up a number of 1.5-yard-wide gates randomly arranged in your grid. The size and number of gates can vary depending on the number of pairs of players you have and their skill level. I would start with at least as many gates as pairs. Players score a point for each completed pass they make through a gate to their partner. Go for 30-45 seconds and have pairs keep count of how many points they get. See how many they get and ask how the top pair got so many. Get them to demonstrate. Repeat. Switch partners. Repeat. If your players are struggling with this game, make the gates bigger. The objective is simply to get them passing with their partner on the move. You should always start an activity so that everyone can quickly find success. Once they understand the game, that's what you can start to make it progressively more challenging.

Possible Progressions:
- Add a restriction that players must use a certain foot or surface of the foot to make a pass and score a point.
- Replace some of the gates with pinnies (or different colored gates) and say that pairs must go through a cone gate followed by a pinnie/bib gate.
- Make the gates smaller/reduce the number of gates.
- Introduce a bandit (or pair of "bandits") whose job is to stop pairs from scoring in gates. Change the bandit(s).

Activity #1: 4v1

Time: Approximately 15 minutes.

Area: Set up grids of approximately 10 x 10 yards (make bigger if you have weaker players).

Activity: While staying in the grid at all times, 4 players attempt to keep the ball away from 1. Play rounds of 30-45 seconds. When the time is up change the person in the middle. Have each group keep count of the highest number of consecutive passes they managed. The first pass is always "free" (e.g., the defenders must allow it). The group with the lowest number of passes does a quick consequence (e.g., 20 toe taps, 5 knees to chest, 5 sit-ups, etc.).

4v1 is a great warm-up activity for your team. It gets them a lot of touches on the ball, requires them to deal with pressure, and forces them to make decisions. Depending on numbers, you can make it 4v2, or 3v1.

Possible Progressions:

- Put touch restrictions on the players (e.g., 3 touch max, then 2 touch max, then 1 touch).
- Mandate that players must follow their pass (constant movement/chaos).

- Put the attacking team on the outside of the grid with one of them in the middle.
- Mandate that all passes must cross two lines to count (this means that the players keeping the ball must stand outside the grid).

Activity #2: Basic Possession

Time: Approximately 15 minutes

Area: 50 x 60 yards (W x L), or as close to half a game field as you can get. Start big, you can always make it smaller.

Activity: Split players up into two teams of even numbers, with the objective being to keep the ball for as long as possible (a coach can keep count by counting the seconds out loud – I would suggest the first 5 are in your head!). Give them a certain amount of time (e.g., 3 minutes) and then take the highest number of consecutive seconds in possession from each team to declare a winner. If you have a large number of players (e.g., more than 20), you may want to consider using 2 smaller grids (in order to maximize the players' number of touches and learning situations). If you have a smaller number of players (e.g., 12 or less), you may want to make the field smaller.

Possible Progressions:

- Make it so teams score a goal by keeping the ball for 10 seconds. Play first team to score 3 goals, wins.
- Add a neutral(s), so the team in possession always has a slight advantage.
- Put all players on a touch restriction (e.g., 3 touch maximum, 2 touch maximum).
- Add a halfway line and mandate that teams may only starting counting passes that are completed in the opponents' half.

Activity #3: 2v1 Continuous*Wide

Time: Approximately 20 minutes.

Area: If you have a marked 18-yard box, use it and then mark out another one with cones to create a 36 x 44 yard (L x W) playing grid.

Activity: Divide the players into 2 even teams. Have them line up as shown in the diagram above. The balls should be divided equally and diagonally (as per the diagram). To begin, you can play the ball into the middle. Players go to the other line once they have had their turn (e.g., attacker goes to the other attacker line). Any time the ball crosses a line (side, end, goal), the team whose possession it would be restarts the game from their side with a new pair (the defending pair stays in). Also, any time a ball crosses the end line from a shot (including a goal), the shooter must run around the corner while the 2 defenders drop out (the attacking team now becomes the numbers down defending team), and a new attack begins by 2 forwards to make it 2v1 (with the recovering defender who just shot the ball running around the corner). Play first team to a set number of goals (e.g., 5, 7, 9) and give the losing team a consequence. After the consequence, you can ask the guided discovery questions, while the players catch their breath.

This game will take a few rounds for the players to understand. It is very important that you are consistent with the rules. I find it helps to communicate early and often; for example, if the ball goes out of play, I will say "red team's ball." Also, if someone forgets to run, I will remind that player (e.g., "Janie, you have to run"). If she influences the play, I will award a penalty kick to the other team, which will transition back into 2v1 continuous immediately following the kick.

Possible Progressions:

- Move the balls to the other side (move the players, too, so the wide player is always on the "weak side")
- Give 2 points for first time finishes (encourages combination plays, crosses, etc.).

End of Practice Scrimmage: 2/3 Field Scrimmage

Time: Approximately 30 minutes (or whatever is left of practice).

Area: Using a marked field, make an 18-yard box with cones (using the halfway line as the edge of the box). If you don't have a marked field, make your field as big as you can (but not as long as a game field).

Activity: Play even numbers and arrange teams in a formation that reflects your desired game day formation. By reducing the length of the field, you can get more action by the goal and the players won't get as tired as they would from a full field scrimmage, yet there is still plenty of space in which the players can operate. Using the halfway line as the edge of the 18-yard box also makes the field "look" more like a full size field, with the added benefit of the ball always being closer to the boxes than on a regular field.

Possible Progressions:

- Play that 5 consecutive passes equals a goal (increase the number of passes, as needed, depending on your team's ability).
- Play that 5 consecutive passes in the opponent's half equals a goal (increase the number of passes, as needed, depending on your team's ability).
- Add a neutral(s) to give the team in possession an advantage.
- Put one or both teams on touch restrictions (e.g., 3 touch max, 2 touch max, 1 touch max!).

Session #4: Exploding Past Defenders

This session is designed to introduce your players to the primary role of the first attacker when moving towards goal and confronted by a defender. It is appropriate for any level of player and can also be used at the beginning of the season to make sure all players know the basics of beating a defender in a 1v1 situation.

What will players learn from this session?

- These activities force players to confront a 1v1 battle. The aim is to get the ball past a defender (attacking mindset and penetration).
- Players constantly change pace and direction with the ball in a confined space (mobility).
- Successful players, especially the ones who are not the fastest, will start to disguise their movements (improvisation).
- Successful players keep their heads up and eyes open to see where the space is, but also to recognize the visual cues of the defender (e.g., where is she looking, are they favoring one particular side, are they weak on one side, what is their body position?).

Coaching Points for the session:
Praise players when they engage a defender in a 1v1 battle and try to beat them at pace.

- Praise creativity (even when it doesn't come off).
- Praise players when they disguise their attacking intentions.
- Praise players who change speed and direction to beat a defender.
- Praise players who dribble the ball towards the defender's front foot.

Guided discovery questions for the session: (can be asked at any point)

- Is it easier or harder to beat the defender when you go fast or slow? Why?
- Is it easier or harder to beat the defender when you change pace and direction? Why?
- What kind of moves can you use to be successful? What do you think makes them work?
- How can you read the defender's body language and positioning to know what to do?
- Do you want to take your explosive touch past the defender into a big or a small space? Why?

Warm-up Activity: Sharks and Minnows

Time: Approximately 10 minutes.

Area: Approximately 15 x 15 yards (L x W) - the grid's size depends on your numbers (how big/small you want to make it). Remember, making it bigger will make it easier for the minnows (attackers). If you have large numbers, consider making two (or more) grids (and splitting by ability).

Activity: The minnows each have a ball and their task is to stay inside the grid and not have the shark(s) kick their ball out. Select a pair of sharks. Once a minnow has her ball kicked out, she must retrieve it and perform a certain number of toe taps (or tic tocs with the insides of her feet) before she can return to the grid (base this on the skill level of your group). The objective is for the sharks to clear the grid of minnows. Once you have demonstrated the role of shark, the kids will all want their turn. Play the game as many times as is necessary to allow all the kids their turn at being a shark (stop games that go on for longer than 45 seconds - or join in and help!). Give the shark a pinnie/bib!

Possible Progressions:

- Change the number of toe taps/insides players have to do.
- Instead of toe taps, have players do a certain number of ball juggles (e.g., 10 "feet only").

- Mandate that players can only use a certain foot (e.g., only left foot or only right foot) in the grid.
- Add a shark(s); make the grid bigger/smaller.

Activity #1: 1v1 Grid

Time: Approximately 20 minutes. How frequently you do this activity with your team (as well as the level of your team), will determine whether you are able to get through none, some, or all of the progressions.

Area: Make a number of 7 x 10 yard (W x L) "tunnels" (can be smaller or bigger depending on how many players you have and their ability levels).

Activity: Divide the players into 2 even teams and split to form 4 groups. Have the defenders line up behind one of the corner cones (with the balls) and have the attackers line up diagonally opposite. The defender passes the ball to the forward and then goes to defend. The attacker scores a point by dribbling past the defender and stopping the ball on the defender's end line (if the defender steals the ball, they can score a point on the opposite end). Give them a time limit (e.g., 75 seconds) to score as many goals as possible (keep count) and then have the two teams switch roles. The losing team faces a consequence. Repeat for a couple of rounds (in order to ask guided discovery questions). My advice would be to play for 2 minutes (players go back to their same line) and then switch roles (e.g., defenders now become attackers and vice versa). One trick here is to have one more player on one of the sides - this means that players will compete against a different person each time.

Possible progressions:

- Change where the defenders and attackers start from on their line (e.g., defenders on the left, forwards central, diagonally across, etc.).
- Add gate goals (a couple of yards wide) in each corner (both ends) - have players dribble through/pass through them to score.
- Replace the corner gates with a central goal (4 yards) at each end.

Activity #2: The End Zone Game

Time: Approximately 15 minutes.

Area: If you have a marked 18-yard box, use it and put a cone 5 yards to the side of each post. If not, make your own and put a cone facing it 18 yards away.

Activity: Divide up the players into two even teams. The coach stands with the balls off to one side (around midfield – see diagram). Teams score a point when they dribble the ball into one of the end zones (they can score in either end zone at any time). Defenders are not allowed in the end zones. Play first team to score 3-5 points, and then review coaching points/ask guided discovery questions as appropriate. Repeat as necessary.

Possible Progressions:

- Mandate that to score, all of a team's players must be in the attacking half.
- Add that if the defending team gets scored on, while one or more of their players is "caught" in the attacking half, the point is doubled (worth 2 points).
- Play transition (when a team scores in one end zone, they can immediately restart going towards the other end zone).
- Add a neutral(s) so that the attacking team always has an advantage.

Activity #3: 1v1 to Goal with Goalkeepers

Time: Approximately 15 minutes.

Area: If you have a marked 18-yard box, use it and then mark out another one with cones to create a 36 x 44 yard (L x W) playing grid.

Activity: Divide the players into 2 even teams. Have the defenders line up behind the 2 cones, level with the posts. Have the attackers line up in 2 short lines opposite them (and level with their own goal line). The balls should be with the attackers. To begin, have one of the attackers dribble towards the goal and try to score. As soon as the attacker takes his/her first touch forwards, the defender can come out to pressure him/her (but not before). By setting up 2 lines, as soon as one side finishes (goal, tackle, takes too long), you can have the opposite forward begin immediately. Players go to the other line once they have had their turn (e.g., attacker goes to the other attacker line and defender goes to the other defender line). Give them a time limit (e.g., 75 seconds) to score as many goals as possible (keep count) and then have the two teams switch roles. The losing team faces a consequence. Repeat for a couple of rounds (in order to ask guided discovery questions) before you introduce the progressions one at a time.

Possible Progressions:

- Change where the defenders and attackers start from on their line (e.g., defenders on the left, forwards diagonally across, etc.).
- Have the defender serve the ball to the forward to begin the activity.
- Have the goalkeeper serve the ball to the forward to begin the activity.
- Have the coach serve the ball to the forward to begin the activity.

End of Practice Scrimmage: Beat the Defender

Time: Approximately 30 minutes (or whatever is left of practice).

Area: One half of the field. Make a halfway line using cones. By putting a Coerver goal on the actual halfway line, you can have two of these scrimmages at the same time. Depending on your numbers, you may want to play the entire width of the field or just the width of the 18-yard box. Typically, I will play the width of the 18 for 5v5 - 7v7; however, if you find that space too restrictive, you can always open it up.

Activity: Players score a point for beating a defender in a 1v1 duel in the attacking half. Regular goals still count (1 point). Play even numbers and arrange teams in a formation that reflects your desired game day formation.

Progressions:

- Take away the goalkeepers (it will encourage players to take more offensive risks).
- Offer a "triple" point option for when a player beats his man 1v1 and then immediately scores in the goal.
- Add a neutral(s) to give the team in possession an advantage.

Session #5: Finishing in the Box

The vast majority of goals are scored within the 18-yard box. The more comfortable your players are in this area, the more it will payoff during games. This session is designed to put your players in shooting scenarios (under pressure) in the 18-yard box. It is appropriate for any level of player and can be used at any point of the season. You can never score too many goals, right?

What will players learn from this session?

- Players must quickly and efficiently try and score a goal while under pressure from onrushing defender(s) (attacking mindset and penetration).
- This session encourages quick combination play and for attackers to follow up all shots for rebounds (attacking mindset, support, improvisation).
- [2v1 Continuous] is organized chaos; it forces players to think and act quickly, coming up with creative solutions to problems "on the fly" (attacking mindset and improvisation).
- While this session focuses on the role of the first attacker (player with the ball), the role of the second attacker comes to the fore, too – they must keep up with play and quickly get into a position that creates a 2v1 "overload" situation (attacking mindset, support, and mobility).

Coaching Points for the session:

- Praise players when they take offensive risks to get a shot away.
- Praise players when they make appropriate shot selection decisions (not the execution/outcome).
- Praise creativity (even when it doesn't come off).
- Praise players when they disguise their intentions.
- Praise players who change speed and direction to escape pressure.
- Praise players who create space for themselves and/or their teammates with clever runs.

Guided discovery questions for the session: (can be asked at any point)

- Is it easier for you to score when you go slow or fast? Why?
- What types of shots (what surface of the foot is best) help you to score the most? Why?
- What is the best way to eliminate the defender from the activity?

- If you pass the ball to your partner(s), what is the best type of pass and why?
- When you receive the ball, where should you look to take your first touch? Why?
- If you lose the ball, what should you immediately do? Why?
- How can you ensure an overload in this game? What about on restarts?
- What types of things can you say to help your teammate(s)? When/why would you say that?

Warm-up Activity: World Cup

Time: Approximately 10 minutes.

Area: In front of a big goal.

Activity: The coach (or someone you designate) goes in goal and it is "every player for herself" trying to score as many goals as possible. The coach has a supply of balls and serves a new ball in as soon as one goes out of play (or behind the goal). Serve the ball into spaces where the majority of players are not, but try to keep everything within the 18-yard box (or equivalent). If the coach is the goalkeeper, then just keep the spare balls in the goal. As more people arrive, make teams of 2 or even 3. Give team names (e.g., England, USA, Brazil, etc.). Play first person or team to 3 goals and then mix up the teams and play again. If you have a player or number of players that are much better than the others, you can put them on special touch restrictions (e.g., two touch, or left foot only), or mandate that they must score more goals to win.

This is a great game to play with any numbers up to about 12 players (in which case, I would go with teams of 3 and/or have 2 balls in play at a time). If you have more, set up a second or even third goal. Alternatively, you incentivize players to come to practice on time/early by having one World Cup field set up and then once that field is full, have a different warm-up activity grid (e.g., a pong championship ladder, 5v2 grid, juggling competition, etc.).

Possible Progressions:

- If you have access to a second goal, set up another "World Cup" (split by ability).
- Put players on touch restrictions (e.g., 3 touch max, 2 touch max, 1 touch max).
- Put in place a "first time finish rule."
- Add a second ball (this can get crazy, but it adds an extra spark).

Activity #1: The Penalty Box Shooting Game

Time: Approximately 20 minutes.

Area: Utilize the 18-yard box – the "penalty box." The dimensions are 18 x 44 yards (W x L).

Activity: Put a cone on each side of the goal line (about 5-6 yards off of each post). Divide players into 2 or 3 teams (if you have more than 8 players it is usually better to go with 3 teams). Assuming 3 teams, 1 team defends (they will start behind the two goal line cones), 1 team will retrieve and replace balls, and the other team will be shooting. All of the balls need to be put outside the 18-yard box (about a yard or two off of the line). The rules are simple: All attackers must start inside the box. Only 1 attacker may leave to get a ball. As soon as (s)he touches the ball, 1 defender may enter the box to try stop the attacking team from scoring. Only 1 ball and 1 defender are allowed in the box at a time. Any time an attacker shoots, she must run to the nearest goal post and touch it with her hand (this encourages follow up shots as well as adding a natural "point" to the attack). Allow a couple of minutes for players to figure out the rules and rhythms of the game, then give each attacking team 75 seconds to score as many goals as possible. Rotate the attacking team to defense, defense to ball retrieval, and ball retrieval to attacking. Repeat again so that all three teams get to go at all three roles. If you have the players and another goal, set up another field (4 per team, 2 teams on each field).

Possible Progressions:

- Mandate that the ball must be passed into the box before someone can shoot.
- Allow 2 defenders in at a time.
- Disperse the balls evenly around the entire box (instead of just on the sides/front).
- Mandate that all shots must be "first time."
- Move the balls to the sides rather than the front of the box.

Activity #2: Outside In

Time: Approximately 20 minutes.

Area: If you have a marked 18-yard box, use it and then mark out another one with cones to create a 36 x 44 yards (L x W) playing grid.

Activity: Divide the players into 2 even (ability) teams with a goalkeeper in each goal. Send two players from each team outside the grid (as per the diagram). The balls should be divided evenly and placed with the players from each team on the outside of the grid. The players on the outside serve the ball into play (take it in turns) when the ball goes out of play. Play first team to a set number of goals (e.g., 2, 3) and then switch the outside players. The idea is that the outside player will play a pass to a teammate who can then quickly get a shot away on goal.

Possible Progressions:

- Give 2 points for each goal that comes from an outside player.
- Add the number of outside servers.
- Put all players inside the grid on a touch restriction (e.g., 2 touch maximum).
- Mandate that all goals must be a first time finish.

Activity #3: 2v1 Continuous*Stacked

Time: Approximately 20 minutes.

Area: If you have a marked 18-yard box, use it and then mark out another one with cones to create a 36 x 44 yard (L x W) playing grid.

Activity: Divide the players into 2 even teams. Have one team line up opposite each other (see the diagram) behind the 2 cones level with the edge of the 6-yard box. Have the other team do the same on the other side. The balls should be divided equally and diagonally (per the diagram). To begin, you can play the ball into the middle. Players go to the other line once they have had their turn (e.g., attacker goes to the other attacker line). Any time the ball crosses a line (side, end, goal), the team whose possession it would be restarts the game from their side with a new pair (the defending pair stays in). Also, any time a ball crosses the end line from a shot (including a goal), the shooter must run around the corner while the 2 defenders drop out (the attacking team now becomes the numbers down defending team), and a new attack begins by 2 forwards to make it 2v1 (with the recovering defender who just shot the ball running around the corner). Play first team to a set number of goals (e.g., 5, 7, 9) and give the losing team a consequence. After the consequence, you can ask the guided discovery questions, while the players catch their breath. This game will take a few rounds for the players to understand. It is very important that you are consistent with the rules. I find it helps to communicate early and often; for example, if the ball goes out of play, I will say "red team's ball." Also, if someone forgets to run, I will remind that player (e.g., "Janie, you have to run"). If she influences the play, I will award a penalty kick to the other team, which will transition back into 2v1 continuous immediately following the kick.

Possible Progressions:

- Move the balls to the other side (move the players, too, so the wide player is always on the "weak side").
- Give 2 points for first time finishes (encourages combination plays, crosses, etc.).

End of Practice Scrimmage: Two Touch Inside the Box

Time: Approximately 30 minutes (or whatever is left of practice).

Area: One half of the field (playing to one big goal). By putting a Coerver goal on the halfway line, you can have two of these scrimmages at the same time. Depending on your numbers, you may want to play the entire width of the field or just the width of the 18-yard box. Typically, I will play the width of the 18 for 5v5 - 7v7; however, if you find that space too restrictive, you can always open it up.

Activity: Attacking players have a maximum of two touches inside the box (including a shot!). Play even numbers and arrange teams in a formation that reflects your desired game day formation. For example, if you are playing 8v8, you can put teams in a 3-3-1 formation (this gives you central players as well as wide players on both defense and offense). Alternately, you can set up one (or both) of the teams in a 2-3-2 formation to change things up. This is a good game to play if you have the space and the numbers. If you don't, no need to worry, just divide up the players into two even teams and let them play in the space you do have available.

Progressions:

- Take away the goalkeepers (will encourage players to take offensive risks and lots of shots!).
- Make a rule where teams get double points for first time finishes in the box.
- Add a neutral(s) to give the team in possession an advantage.
- Put one or both teams on touch restrictions (e.g., 3 touch max, 2 touch max, 1 touch max!).

Session #6: The Give and Go

The "give and go" or the "wall pass" is one of the simplest but most effective offensive combination plays in soccer. I prefer to call it the "give and go" because it more accurately describes the action you want to see as opposed to the type of pass (wall). Sometimes players think that the pass is enough and then jog to get the return ball. Emphasize the "go" and they will soon pick it up! This session is appropriate for any age/level and can be modified as needed.

What will players learn from this session?

- Players work together to beat the defense and accomplish their objective (attacking mindset).
- Players constantly change pace and direction with the ball in a confined space (mobility).
- For the second attacker (the player with the ball is always the first attacker) to be effective, she must take up positions to create and maximize the available space (support and width).
- Successful players, especially the ones who are not the fastest, will start to disguise their movements (improvisation).
- Successful players keep their head up and eyes open to see where the space is, but also to recognize the visual cues of the defender(s) (e.g., where is she looking, are they favoring one particular side, are they weak on one side, what is their body position?).

Coaching Points for the session:

- Praise players who change speed and direction to attempt a give and go.
- Praise players when they make appropriate decisions about when and where to try a give and go (not the execution/outcome).
- Praise creativity (even when it doesn't come off).
- Praise players when they disguise their intentions.
- Praise players when they use the give and go as a decoy.
- Praise players who create space for themselves and/or their teammates with clever runs.

Guided discovery questions for the session: (can be asked at any point)

- Is it easier to beat the defender when you go slow or fast? Why?
- How can you "draw the defender in"? Show me.
- When is it not appropriate to do the give and go? Why?

- Is it easier or harder to beat the defender when you change pace and direction?
- If you pass the ball to your partner, what is the best type of pass and why?
- When you receive the ball, where should you look to take your first touch? Why?
- What else can you do in this game to be successful? Explain that to me.

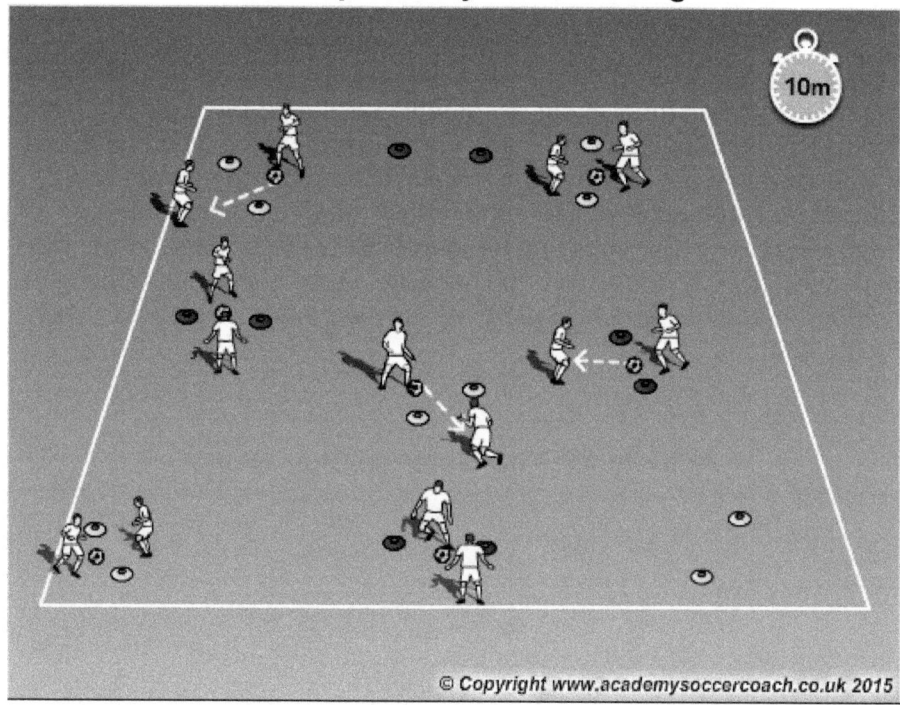

Warm-up Activity: Soccer Pong

Time: Approximately 10 minutes

Area: Big open space

Activity: Two players play against each other and share a ball. They place two cones anywhere from 2-5 yards apart. Players pass back and forth to each other. The rules are that the ball must never stop, must always stay on the ground and must go through the two cones without touching them. Whenever this is violated the other person receives a point. Because of the rule that the ball must never stop, players have to play 1-2 touch. The closer the two cones are the closer the pairs are probably going to be. The farther apart they are, the more they will have to move laterally and look more like the old arcade "pong" game. Play for a specified length of time (e.g., 60 seconds) and see which pair can become the champions. If your players are struggling with this game, make the gates bigger and/or mandate that each player takes two touches (this will slow the game down some, but will reduce the number of mistakes when players attempt to be too aggressive). The objective is simply to get them passing with their partner and working on their first touch.

Possible Progressions:
- Make a "ladder" and after each game have players move up and down if they win/lose.
- Impose a maximum touch limitation (e.g., 2 touches, or 1 touch).
- Change the width of the gates.

*The higher the level of your team's players, the sooner they will figure out how to "game the system" by standing closer to the gate and hitting the ball as hard as they can. If you find this happening, you can make it a cooperative game by having the players count the number of passes they can achieve back and forth through the gate. This happened to me. By modifying the game, we were still able to get lots of passes back and forth through the gate. I also started mandating the number of touches and how far away they were from the gate to vary the game.

Activity #1: The Gate Passing Game

Time: Approximately 15 minutes.

Area: 25x25 yards (L x W) or larger, depending on how many players you have.

Activity: Put players in pairs with a ball. Set up a number of 1.5-yard-wide gates randomly arranged in your grid. The size and number of gates can vary depending on the number of pairs of players you have and their skill level. I would start with at least as many gates as pairs. Players score a point for each completed pass they make through a gate to their partner. Go for 30-45 seconds and have pairs keep count of how many points they get. See how many they get and ask how the top pair got so many. Get them to demonstrate. Repeat. Switch partners. Repeat. If your players are struggling with this game, make the gates bigger. The objective is simply to get them passing with their partner on the move. You should always start an activity so that everyone can quickly find success. Once they understand the game, that's when you can start to make it progressively more challenging.

Possible Progressions:
- Add restriction that players must use a certain foot or surface of the foot to make a pass and score a point.
- Replace some of the gates with pinnies (or different colored gates) and say that pairs must go through a cone gate followed by a pinnie/bib gate.
- Make the gates smaller/reduce the number of gates.
- Introduce a bandit (or pair of "bandits") whose job is to stop pairs from scoring in gates. Change the bandit(s).

Activity #2: The Nickens

Time: Approximately 15 minutes.

Area: Square grid of about 12 x 12 yards (W x L). You can make your grid(s) smaller or bigger depending on how many players you have and their ability levels.

Activity: This game works best when you have different color cones, but it works just fine if you don't. Two teams line up diagonally opposite from each other (per the diagram above). One team has the balls. One player passes the ball to the attacker on the other team, then goes to defend him. Upon receiving the ball, the attacker attempts to dribble the ball through one of the offensive gates in front of him. If the defender steals the ball, he can then try to counter attack and dribble through one of his offensive gates. Go for 60-90 seconds (keeping score) and then swap roles. Whichever team scores the most goals, wins. This is a good activity to see how players solve offensive problems in tight spaces. Alternatively, you can have the attacker start with the ball. Depending on the ability levels of your players, you may want to reduce the number of variables (e.g., the defender's pass to the attacker may disrupt the flow of the activity if he isn't able to pass the ball accurately and consistently).

Possible Progressions:

- First time finishes count double (this will encourage combination plays, such as the give and go/wall pass).
- Make the gates bigger/smaller.
- Make the grid bigger/smaller.

* This activity could become a staple in your coaching repertoire because it offers the basic principles of attack: penetration, change of speed/direction, width, mobility, and creativity. It also contains the basic principles of defense: pressure, cover, move feet, patience/delay, with emphasis on poke tackles.

Activity #3: 2v1 Continuous*Side by Side

Time: Approximately 20 minutes.

Area: If you have a marked 18-yard box, use it and then mark out another one with cones to create a 36 x 44 yard (L x W) playing grid.

Activity: Divide the players into 2 even teams. Have one team line up behind the 2 cones level with the edge of the 6-yard box. Have the other team line up in 2 lines on the edge of the opposite box (far cones) facing them. The balls should be divided equally and diagonally (per the diagram). To begin, you can play the ball into the middle.

Players go to the other line once they have had their turn (e.g., attacker goes to the other attacker line). Any time the ball crosses a line (side, end, goal), the team whose possession it would be restarts the game from their side with a new pair (the defending pair stays in). Also, any time a ball crosses the end line from a shot (including a goal), the shooter must run around the corner while the 2 defenders drop out (the attacking team now becomes the numbers down defending team), and a new attack begins with 2 forwards to make it 2v1 (with the recovering defender who just shot the ball running around the corner). Play first team to a set number of goals (e.g., 5, 7, 9) and give the losing team a consequence. After the consequence, you can ask the guided discovery questions, while the players catch their breath. This game will take a few rounds for the players to understand. It is very important that you are consistent with the rules. I find it helps to communicate early and often; for example, if the ball goes out of play, I will say "red team's ball." Also, if someone forgets to run, I will remind that player (e.g., "Janie, you have to run"). If she influences the play, I will award a penalty kick to the other team, which will transition back into 2v1 continuous immediately following the kick.

Possible Progressions:

- Move the balls to the other side (move the players, too, so the wide player is always on the "weak side").
- Give 2 points for first time finishes (encourages combination plays, crosses, etc.).

End of Practice Scrimmage: Beat the Offside Line

Time: Approximately 30 minutes (or whatever is left of practice).

Area: Using a full field (or as much space as you have available), mark an offside line on each end of the field (per the diagram above).

Activity: The only way the attacking team can break the offside line is to play a first time pass into that zone (e.g. a give and go). Defenders are not allowed behind the offside line until the play has been played. This creates an advantage to the attacking team and will result in a lot of breakaways (1v1 to goal). Play even numbers and arrange teams in a formation that reflects your desired game day formation. For example, if you are playing 8v8, you can put teams in a 3-3-1 formation (this gives you central players as well as wide players on both defense and offense). Alternately, you can set up one (or both) of the teams in a 2-3-2 formation to change things up.

Possible Progressions:

- Allow double the points for goals scored immediately following a give and go.
- Add a neutral(s) to give the team in possession an advantage.
- Put one or both teams on touch restrictions (e.g., 3 touch max, 2 touch max, 1 touch max!).

Session #7: Introduction to Scoring Goals in Transition

Even though it has been around since the beginning of soccer, "transition" has been one of the buzzwords of the last few years. Essentially, "transition" occurs at the point you win/lose the ball. As we are focusing on offense, for our purposes, we will use transition to mean the point at which we win the ball back from the other team. Usually, this is a critical moment because the other team is not defensively "set up" which means there is more space and opportunity than usual. This session is designed to allow your players to look for and take advantage of these situations.

What will players learn from this session?
- Players constantly change pace and direction going to goal in a confined space (mobility).
- Playing at speed as soon as they win the ball, gives players more opportunity to score (attacking mindset).
- Successful players, especially the ones who are not the fastest, will start to disguise their movements (improvisation).
- Successful players keep their head up and eyes open to see where the space is, but also to recognize the visual cues of the defender(s) (e.g., where is she looking, are they favoring one particular side, are they weak on one side, what is their body position?).
- Successful players will utilize combination plays, such as wall passes, overlaps, and takeovers, or they will "fake" them to gain advantage and create an opportunity (mobility and improvisation).
- This session also encourages players to switch the point of the attack to a less well-defended area in order to exploit the "weak" side (width and improvisation).

Coaching Points for the session:
- Praise players when they are direct (going straight to goal and trying to score as quickly as possible) following transition.
- Praise players who change speed and direction in order to exploit a transitional moment.
- Praise players when they make appropriate decisions about when and where to try to exploit a transitional moment (not the execution/outcome).
- Praise creativity (even when it doesn't come off).
- Praise players when they disguise their intentions.

- Praise players who create space for themselves and/or their teammates with clever runs.

Guided discovery questions for the session: (can be asked at any point)

- What is the first question you should ask yourself when you have the ball?
- Is it easier to beat the defender when you go slow or fast? Why?
- How can you "draw the defender in"? Show me.
- When is it appropriate to dribble/pass? Why? Explain that to me.
- If you pass the ball to your partner, what is the best type of pass and why?
- When you receive the ball, where should you look to take your first touch? Why?
- What else can you do in this game to be successful? Explain that to me.
- How can you best exploit the other team's weakness when they lose the ball? Explain that to me.

Warm-up Activity: The Nickens in Transition

Time: Approximately 15 minutes.

Area: Square grid of about 12 x 12 yards (W x L). You can make your grid(s) smaller or bigger depending on how many players you have and their ability levels.

Activity: This game works best when you have different color cones, but it works just fine if you don't. Arrange the teams as per the diagram above. It works best with 12 players. It is 2v2 in the grid, with both teams having two "goals". A team scores a point by passing the ball to a teammate who is stood behind one of the two gates. At this moment, that player brings that ball into the grid and everyone else in the grid leaves. The attacking team brings in another player from the opposite line and the defending team brings in a new pair of defenders (one from each line). If the ball goes out of bounds (e.g. an inaccurate pass, or a tackle), the team that should have possession gets a ball from one of their outside players and plays on, but the only way a pair leaves the grid is when they (or the other pair) score. The game will be a bit chaotic at first, but that is the nature of transition – we are looking for quick, decisive play.

Possible Progressions:

- First time passes through the gate count double (this will encourage combination plays, such as the give and go/wall pass).
- Make the gates bigger/smaller.
- Make the grid bigger/smaller.

Activity #1: Target Ball in Transition

Time: Approximately 20 minutes.

Area: 40 x 50 yards (W x L) - make as big as possible! In the diagram above, I make use of existing lines.

Activity: Put a cone in each corner of the field, then 2 or 3 others (equally distributed) along each end line (see diagram). Balance a ball on top of each cone on the end line. Divide players into 2 teams. The objective is to successfully knock a ball off the cone (with the game ball). When this happens, the attacking team immediately retrieves a ball and can attack the other end (both teams switch the direction in which they are shooting). If a player shoots and misses, (s)he must run to retrieve the ball, while the defending team can take the ball off the cone that the attacker missed (meaning that they will be temporarily "numbers up"). Play first team to 3 goals, then review the guided discovery questions and move through progressions. If defenders are just standing by cones, say that 5 consecutive passes equals a goal. This should entice the defending team to come out and play.

Depending on your numbers (e.g., if you have 16 or more), you may want to go for two smaller fields in order to maximize players' touches on the ball and exposure to learning situations. It is best to experiment and see what works best for your group.

Possible Progressions:

- Add a halfway line and mandate that, to score, all of the attacking team's players must be in the attacking half.
- Add a neutral(s), so that the attacking team is always at an advantage.
- Put all players on a touch restriction (e.g., 3 touch maximum).
- Finally, mandate that "goals" must be first time (e.g., players must knock the ball off the cone with their first touch!).

Activity #2: 2v1 Continuous*Side by Side

Time: Approximately 20 minutes.

Area: If you have a marked 18-yard box, use it and then mark out another one with cones to create a 36 x 44 yard (L x W) playing grid.

Activity: Divide the players into 2 even teams. Have one team line up behind the 2 cones, level with the edge of the 6-yard box. Have the other team line up in 2 lines on the edge of the opposite box (far cones) facing them. The balls should be divided equally and diagonally (per the diagram). To begin, you can play the ball into the middle. Players go to the other line once they have had their turn (e.g., attacker goes to the other attacker line). Any time the ball crosses a line (side, end, goal), the team whose possession it would be restarts the game from their side with a new pair of attackers (the defending pair stays in). Also, any time a ball crosses the end line from a shot (including a goal), the shooter must run around the corner while the 2 defenders drop out (the attacking team now becomes the numbers down defending team), and a new attack begins by 2 forwards to make it 2v1 (whilst the recovering defender who just shot the ball is running around the corner). Play first team to a set number of goals (e.g., 5, 7, 9) and give the losing team a consequence. After the consequence, you can ask the guided discovery questions, while the players catch their breath. This game will take a few rounds for the players to understand. It is very important that you are consistent with the rules. I find it helps to communicate early and often; for example, if the ball goes out of play, I will say "yellow team's ball." Also, if someone forgets to run, I will remind that player (e.g., "Gareth, you have to run"). If Gareth influences the play, I will award a penalty kick to the other team, which will transition back into 2v1 continuous immediately following the kick.

Possible Progressions:

- Move the balls to the other side (move the players, too, so the wide player is always on the "weak side").
- Give 2 points for first time finishes (encourages combination plays, crosses, etc.).

Activity #3: 3v2 Continuous*Stacked and Wide

Time: Approximately 20 minutes.

Area: If you have a marked 18-yard box, use it and then mark out another one with cones to create a 36 x 44 yard (L x W) playing grid.

Activity: Divide the players into 2 even teams. Have them line up as shown in the diagram above. The balls should be divided equally and diagonally (per the diagram). There should be 3 players from each team in the grid (a player from each line). To begin the game, you can play the ball into the middle, or give the ball to one of the players. Players go to a different line once they have had their turn (e.g., attacker from the ball line goes to the wide line). Any time the ball crosses a line (side, end, goal), the team whose possession it would be restarts the game from their side with a new attacking trio (the defending trio stays in). Also, any time a ball crosses the end line from a shot (including a goal), the shooter must run around the corner while the 3 defenders drop out (the attacking team now becomes the numbers down defending team), and a new attack begins with 3 forwards to make it 3v2 (with the recovering defender who just shot the ball running around the corner). Play first team to a set number of goals (e.g., 5, 7, 9) and give the losing team a consequence. After the consequence, you can ask the guided discovery questions, while the players catch their breath.

This game looks (and is!) chaotic; however, once players get used to the rules, it provides great teachable moments for integrating width and depth into attacking movements in a fast-paced, continuous environment.

Possible Progressions:

- Move the balls to the other side (move the players, too, so the wide player is always on the "weak side").
- Give 2 points for first time finishes (encourages combination plays, crosses, etc.).

End of Practice Scrimmage: Half Field Transition

Time: Approximately 30 minutes (or whatever is left of practice).

Area: One half of the field (playing to one big goal). By putting a Coerver goal on the halfway line, you can have two of these scrimmages at the same time. Depending on your numbers, you may want to play the entire width of the field or just the width of the 18-yard box. Typically, I will play the width of the 18 for 5v5 - 7v7; however, if you find that space too restrictive, you can always open it up.

Activity: The goalkeepers are fixed at each end (i.e. they are not assigned to either team). As soon as a team scores in one goal, it retains possession of the ball and can immediately attack the opposite goal (both teams switch the direction they are shooting at this point). Play even numbers and arrange teams in a formation that reflects your desired game day formation.

Progressions:

- Add a neutral(s) to give the team in possession an advantage.
- Put one or both teams on touch restrictions (e.g., 3 touch max, 2 touch max, 1 touch max!).

Session #8: Scoring with the Laces

Striking the ball with the laces is essential at any level of soccer, but, in my experience, it is a skill that is often overlooked by coaches. Having players with the ability to strike the ball accurately and with power will create lots of opportunities for your team. This session is designed to introduce players to how they should be striking the ball with their laces, when and where it might be appropriate, and what the benefits are. It is appropriate for all ages and skill levels.

What will players learn from this session?

- The best technique for consistently striking the ball with the laces.
- How to develop "muscle memory" for the correct technique (this will need to be built up over time).
- "Sorting their feet out" – meaning how to approach the ball before striking it.

Coaching Points for the session:
Praise players when they lock their ankle and keep their toe pointed.

- Praise players when they try to approach the ball at an angle (around 45 degrees) and get their "plant" (non-kicking) foot out of the way to allow a clean, smooth strike.
- Praise players when they strike the ball cleanly REGARDLESS of where the ball ends up.
- Praise players when they attempt to use the laces technique with their non-dominant foot.

Guided discovery questions for the session: (can be asked at any point)

- Why do you think you are supposed to keep your ankle locked and toe pointed when you strike the ball?
- Why do you think you are supposed to approach the ball at an angle?
- How can you best position your non-kicking foot to set you up for a clean strike every single time?
- Is it easier or harder to strike the ball cleanly when you try and hit it your hardest? Why do you think that is? What does this mean you should try to do instead?
- When and where might you employ the laces technique for shooting? Why?
- How else might the laces technique be useful?

Warm-up Activity: The Circle Game

Time: Approximately 20 minutes.

Area: Put players in a circle whose radius is 10-12 yards (a center circle is 10 yards). An easy way to create a circle is by putting down a cone, walking out 10-12 yards at 4 points, and telling the players to make a circle around the 4 "point" cones.

Activity: Have the players get in a circle. There should be equal spacing between each player. For organizational purposes, create 2 groups. Number each player 1 or 2 (should be an equal number of each). Have the group of 1s come to the middle of the circle; the 2s are on the outside. The 2s should have a ball in their hands. Once the game gets going, there are simply players in the middle receiving and passing and players on the outside who are passing and receiving. Working in intervals of 30-45 seconds, the outside players throw the ball (underarm) to players in the middle whose job it is volley it right back to the passer first time (with the laces). Have the inside players keep count of their completed volleys. If you feel it is appropriate, have the person with the fewest passes do a quick (5 second) consequence on the outside of the circle. In order to improve technique, players need repetitions. In this activity, players work under increasingly game-like conditions as pressure and difficulty intensify. Ensure that they are checking for the ball at speed to begin with (later on, if they don't, they will never get the ball!).

Possible Progressions:

- Mandate a certain foot; e.g., right foot, then only left foot, then either foot.
- Mandate players in the middle take two touches: thigh control, laces volley back.
- Mandate players in the middle take two touches: chest control, laces volley back.
- Take away a ball (creates competition in the middle for a ball; leads to receiving under pressure).
- Take away another ball (intensifies the above).

Activity #1: The Penalty Box Shooting Game

Time: Approximately 20 minutes.

Area: Utilize the 18-yard box – the "penalty box." The dimensions are 18 x 44 yards (W x L).

Activity: Put a cone on each side of the goal line (about 5-6 yards off each post). Divide players into 2 or 3 teams (if you have more than 8 players it is usually better to go with 3 teams). Assuming 3 teams, 1 team defends (they will start behind the two goal line cones), 1 team will retrieve and replace balls, and the other team will be shooting. All of the balls need to be outside the 18-yard box about a yard or two off the line. The rules are simple: All attackers must start inside the box. Only 1 attacker may leave to get a ball. As soon as she touches the ball, 1 defender may enter the box to try to stop the attacking team from scoring. Only 1 ball and 1 defender are allowed in the box at a time. Any time an attacker shoots, she must run to the nearest goal post and touch it with her hand (this encourages shot follow up as well as adding a natural "point" to the attack). Allow a couple of minutes for players to figure out the rules and rhythms of the game, then give each attacking team 75 seconds to score as many goals as possible. Rotate attacking team to defense, defense to ball retrieval, and ball retrieval to attacking. Repeat again so that all three teams get a go at all three roles. If you have the players and another goal, set up another field (4 per team, 2 teams on each field).

Possible Progressions:

- Mandate that the ball must be passed into the box before someone can shoot.
- Allow 2 defenders in at a time.
- Disperse the balls evenly around the entire box (instead of just on the sides/front).
- Mandate that all shots must be "first time."
- Move the balls to the sides rather than the front of the box.

Activity #2: 6v6 Plus 6

Time: Approximately 20 minutes.

Area: If you have a marked 18-yard box, use it and then mark out another one with cones to create a 36 x 44 yards (L x W) playing grid. Add a halfway line (as shown in the diagram above).

Activity: This game works best with 20 players (2 goalkeepers and 18 outfield players), but can easily be modified to fit your numbers. Divide the players into 3 even (ability) teams with a goalkeeper in each goal. The balls should be divided evenly and placed in each goal for quick and easy retrieval by the goalkeeper. The players on the team that is "out", position themselves around the edge of the field (1 on each long side, and 1 either side of each goal). These players serve as "bumpers," have 1 touch, and play on whichever team passes them the ball – in essence, they are neutrals. There are no offsides in this game. Play first team to a set number of goals (e.g., 2, 3) and give the losing team a consequence. The losing team then switches with the "bumper" team.

Possible Progressions:

- Give 2 points for each goal that comes from behind the halfway line.
- Put all players inside the grid on a touch restriction (e.g., 3 touch maximum).
- Mandate that all goals must be a first time finish.

Activity #3: 2v1 Continuous*Stacked

Time: Approximately 20 minutes.

Area: If you have a marked 18-yard box, use it and then mark out another one with cones to create a 36 x 44 yard (L x W) playing grid.

Activity: Divide the players into 2 even teams. Have one team line up opposite each other (see the diagram) behind the 2 cones, level with the edge of the 6-yard box. Have the other team do the same on the other side. The balls should be divided equally and diagonally (per the diagram). To begin, you can play the ball into the middle. Players go to the other line once they have had their turn (e.g., attacker goes to the other attacker line). Any time the ball crosses a line (side, end, goal), the team whose possession it would be restarts the game from their side with a new attacking pair (the defending pair stays in). Also, any time a ball crosses the end line from a shot (including a goal), the shooter must run around the corner while the 2 defenders drop out (the attacking team now becomes the numbers down defending team), and a new attack begins with 2 forwards to make it 2v1 (with the recovering defender who just shot the ball running around the corner). Play first team to a set number of goals (e.g., 5, 7, 9) and give the losing team a consequence. After the consequence, you can ask the guided discovery questions, while the players catch their breath.

This is a great activity to teach your players the importance of attacking at speed, isolating a single defender, and where/when the supporting attacker should make his run.

Possible Progressions:
- Move the balls to the other side (move the players, too, so the wide player is always on the "weak side").
- Give 2 points for first time finishes (encourages combination plays, crosses, etc.).

End of Practice Scrimmage: Half Field Scrimmage

Time: Approximately 30 minutes (or whatever is left of practice).

Area: One half of the field (playing to one big goal). By putting a Coerver goal on the halfway line, you can have two of these scrimmages at the same time. Depending on your numbers, you may want to play the entire width of the field or just the width of the 18-yard box. Typically, I will play the width of the 18 for 5v5 - 7v7; however, if you find that space too restrictive, you can always open it up.

Activity: As per the diagram, put in a halfway line and state that all goals from behind the halfway line count for double. Play even numbers and arrange teams in a formation that reflects your desired game day formation. For example, if you are playing 8v8, you can put teams in a 3-3-1 formation (this gives you central players as well as wide players on both defense and offense). Alternately, you can set up one (or both) of the teams in a 2-3-2 formation to change things up. This is a good game to play if you have the space and the numbers. If you don't, no need to worry, just divide up the players into two even teams and let them play in the space you do have available.

Progressions:

- Take away the goalkeepers (will encourage players to take offensive risks and make it easier to score double points).
- Add a neutral(s) to give the team in possession an advantage.

- Put one or both teams on touch restrictions (e.g., 3 touch max, 2 touch max, 1 touch max!).

Session #9: Creating Opportunities from Wide Areas

Having players that can create scoring opportunities when the ball is wide is a great asset. Even at the highest levels of the professional game, disorganized defenses struggle when the ball gets played wide and crossed (or if a team demonstrates that they can create opportunities from wide areas – it creates more space in central areas). This session is designed to introduce your players to the roles of the wide players and the roles of the other attacking players. It is appropriate for any level of player and can be modified to meet the needs of your team.

What will players learn from this session?

- Because the aim of this session is to score a goal when the ball goes wide, players are encouraged to figure out "what works best" when the ball is in wide positions (attacking mindset and penetration).
- The supporting attackers must offer effective angles of support and get into good shooting positions (support, width, and mobility).
- Because the ball is often served from a wide position into the box, forwards must come up with creative finishing solutions in order to score goals (improvisation).
- This session also encourages players to switch the point of the attack to a less well-defended area in order to exploit the "weak" side (width and improvisation).

Coaching Points for the session:

- Praise players when they are direct (going straight to goal and trying to score as quickly as possible) following transition.
- Praise players who change speed and direction in order to exploit a transitional moment.
- Praise players when they make appropriate decisions about when and where to try to create a scoring opportunity when the ball is wide (not the execution/outcome).
- Praise creativity (even when it doesn't come off).
- Praise players when they disguise their intentions.
- Praise players who create space for themselves and/or their teammates with clever runs.
- Praise appropriate runs by forwards (near post, back post, top of the box, etc.).
- Praise communication between players as they figure out who goes where and when.

Guided discovery questions for the session: (can be asked at any point)

- When is it appropriate to dribble/pass? Why? Explain that to me.
- Where should the winger take their first touch? Why? Show me.
- What runs should the forward(s) make? Why? Show me.
- Should the attacking team play fast or slow? Why?
- How do the number and positions of the defenders affect this game? Why?
- How do we play to the biggest advantage to exploit the weakness of the defense? Explain this to me.

Warm-up Activity: Headers and Volleys

Time: Approximately 10 minutes.

Area: In front of a big goal.

Activity: The coach (or someone you designate) goes in goal and it is "every player for herself" trying to score as many goals as possible with only a header or a first time volley (striking the ball in the air without it touching the ground before it reaches the player). As more people arrive, make teams of 2 or even 3. Give team names (e.g.,

England, USA, Brazil, etc.). Play first person or team to 3 goals and then mix up the teams and play again. If you have a player or number of players that are much better than the others, you can put them on special touch restrictions (e.g., two touch, or left foot only), or mandate that they must score more goals to win.

This is a great game to play with any numbers up to about 12 players (in which case, I would go with teams of 3 and/or have 2 balls in play at a time). If you have more, set up a second or even third goal. Alternatively, you can incentivize players to come to practice on time/early by having one World Cup field set up and then once that field is full, have a different warm-up activity grid (e.g., a pong championship ladder, 5v2 grid, juggling competition, etc.).

Possible Progressions:

- If you have access to a second goal, set up another "World Cup" (split by ability).
- Add a second ball (this can get crazy, but it adds an extra spark).

Activity #1: Introduction to the Crossing Game

Time: Approximately 15 minutes.

Area: 50 x 30 yards (W x L)

Activity: Set up a cone on the angle of the six-yard box and end line on both sides (these will be the starting points for your defenders). Set up a cone on each side of the field about 5 yards in from the sideline and about 30 yards from the goal line (these will be the starting points for your crossers). Set up 2 cones about 12 yards back from the 18-yard box, centered and with approximately 10 yards between them (these will be the starting points for the forwards). Finally, set up 2 cones 5 yards behind the last set of cones (this is where extra players will wait). Assign 6 defenders and a goalkeeper. Two defenders stand behind each cone, level with the goal line. The balls should be evenly split up and at the wide positions.

Upon the coach's signal, one of the wide players dribbles the ball toward the goal. When she takes her first touch, the defender on her side comes out to defend her; meanwhile the 2 forwards are also in play and they play 3v1 to goal. When the ball goes out of bounds, the crosser goes to the forward line, while one of the forwards goes to the crosser line. The forward who remains a forward goes to the back of the other forward line. As soon as the ball goes out of play, the coach signals for play to begin from the other side of the field.
This is a fast-paced activity, so have rounds of 75-90 seconds and then change the defenders. Set the attacking team a target (e.g. they have to score 3 goals in 90 seconds); if they meet the target, then the defenders and goalkeeper have a consequence, but if they don't meet the target, then the attacking team has a consequence.

Start with 3v1 and an attainable target so the attacking team finds success early. Between rounds, ask the defending team where they think they should be showing the winger. Similarly, ask the attacking players what runs they could/should be making to make the most of their numerical advantage.

Activity #2: 2v1 Continuous*Ball Starts Wide

Time: Approximately 20 minutes.

Area: If you have a marked 18-yard box, use it and then mark out another one with cones to create a 36 x 44 yard (L x W) playing grid.

Activity: Divide the players into 2 even teams. Have them line up as shown in the diagram above. The balls should be divided equally and with the wide players (per the diagram). To begin, you can play the ball into the middle. Players go to the other line once they have had their turn (e.g., attacker goes to the winger line). Any time the ball crosses a line (side, end, goal), the team whose possession it would be restarts the game from their side with a new pair (the defending pair stays in). Also, any time a ball crosses the end line from a shot (including a goal), the shooter must run around the corner while the 2 defenders drop out (the attacking team now becomes the numbers down defending team), and a new attack begins with 2 forwards to make it 2v1 (with the recovering defender who just shot the ball running around the corner). Play first team to a set number of goals (e.g., 5, 7, 9) and give the losing team a consequence. After the consequence, you can ask the guided discovery questions, while the players catch their breath.

This game will take a few rounds for the players to understand. It is very important that you are consistent with the rules. Nevertheless, what you will find is that the wide players will quickly learn to immediately take the ball directly to goal and try to score. The nearest defender will react by trying to show that player away from goal, which then makes the timing and position of the supporting attacker's run so important.

Possible Progressions:

- Give 2 points for goals scored from crosses.
- Give 3 points for first time finishes from crosses.

Activity #3: 3v2 Continuous*Ball Starts Wide

Time: Approximately 20 minutes.

Area: If you have a marked 18-yard box, use it and then mark out another one with cones to create a 36 x 44 yard (L x W) playing grid.

Activity: Divide the players into 2 even teams. Have them line up as shown in the diagram above. The balls should be divided equally and given to the wide players (per the diagram). To begin, you can play the ball into the middle. Players go to the other line once they have had their turn (e.g., attacker goes to the other attacker line). Any time the ball crosses a line (side, end, goal), the team whose possession it would be restarts the game from their side with a new trio (the defending trio stays in). Also, any time a ball crosses the end line from a shot (including a goal), the shooter must run around the corner while the 3 defenders drop out (the attacking team now becomes the numbers down defending team), and a new attack begins by 3 forwards to make it 3v2 (with the recovering defender who just shot the ball running around the corner). Play first team to a set number of goals (e.g., 5, 7, 9) and give the losing team a consequence. After the consequence, you can ask the guided discovery questions, while the players catch their breath.

This progression from the previous activity adds a player to each side, which makes it more complex and therefore more difficult to score. Now, you can teach two forwards to make complementary runs when the ball is wide (e.g., one goes near post, the other far post).

Possible Progressions:

- Give 2 points to wide players who go straight to goal and score.
- Give 2 points for goals scored from crosses.
- Give 3 points for first time finishes from crosses.

End of Practice Scrimmage: Get it to the Wingers!

© Copyright www.academysoccercoach.co.uk 2015

Time: Approximately 30 minutes (or whatever is left of practice).

Area: Using a marked field, make an 18-yard box with cones (using the halfway line as the edge of the box). If you don't have a marked field, make your field as big as you can (but not as long as a game field). After that, make a channel 5-7 yards wide on each side of the field.

Activity: Each team will send two players to the channels (one from each team in each channel). Once a player receives the ball in the channel, he may not be tackled (not even by the other player in the channel – this way, it will be easier to send crosses in). Put the channel players on a touch restriction (e.g., 3-5, depending on the level of your players) and switch them at regular intervals (e.g., every 3 minutes). Play even numbers and arrange teams in a formation that reflects your desired game day formation. For example, if you are playing 8v8, you can put teams in a 3-3-1 formation (this gives you central players as well as wide players on both defense and offense). Alternately, you can set up one (or both) of the teams in a 2-3-2 formation to change things up. By reducing the length of the field, you can get more action by the goal and the players won't get as tired as they would from a full field scrimmage, yet there is still plenty of space in which the players can operate.

Possible Progressions:

- Award double points for goals that come directly from a cross.
- Award double points for first time finishes.
- Add a neutral(s) to give the team in possession an advantage.
- Put one or both teams on touch restrictions (e.g., 3 touch max, 2 touch max, 1 touch max!).
- Every time the ball goes out, it is a kicked-in restart – this encourages balls into the box.

Session #10: The Overlap

The overlap is a highly effective yet simple combination play that is great for breaking through tight defenses and creating scoring opportunities. Knowing when and where to overlap can be tricky, though. This session is designed to introduce your players to the overlap and how both the first and second attackers must work together to effectively utilize this combination play. It is appropriate for any level of player and can be modified as needed.

What will players learn from this session?

- Players work together to beat the defense and accomplish their objective (attacking mindset).
- Players constantly change pace and direction with the ball in a confined space (mobility).
- Players will learn where, when, and how to most effectively spring the overlap (attacking mindset, support, penetration).
- Players will learn how to use the overlap as a decoy to create space/a scoring opportunity (improvisation, attacking mindset).
- Successful players, especially the ones who are not the fastest, will look to disguise their movements (improvisation).
- Successful players keep their head up and eyes open to see where the space is, but also to recognize the visual cues of the defender(s) and the situation (e.g., is the defender isolated? Will an overlap create an overload which leads to a scoring opportunity?).

Coaching Points for the session:

- Praise players when they create a better angle for an overlap by taking their first touch in the direction they received the ball from.
- Praise players who change speed and direction to attempt an overlap.
- Praise players when they make appropriate decisions about when and where to try an overlap (not the execution/outcome).
- Praise creativity (even when it doesn't come off).
- Praise players when they disguise their intentions.
- Praise players when they use the overlap as a decoy.
- Praise players who create space for themselves and/or their teammates with clever runs.

Guided discovery questions for the session: (can be asked at any point)

- How can you "draw the defender in"? Show me.

- When you pass the ball to your partner, what is the best type of pass and why?
- When you receive the ball, where should you look to take your first touch in order to create a better angle for an overlap? Why? Show me.
- When making the overlapping run, is it easier to beat the defender when you go slow or fast? Why?
- When you receive the ball "on the overlap," what type of touch should you take and why?
- When is it not appropriate to do the overlap? Why?
- What else can you do in this game to be successful? Explain that to me.

Warm-up Activity: The Circle Game

Time: Approximately 15-20 minutes.

Area: Put players in a circle whose radius is 10-12 yards. An easy way to do this is to put down a cone and then walk out 10-12 yards at 4 points and tell the players to make a circle around the 4 "point" cones.

Activity: Have the players get in a circle (ideally around the centre circle; if there is not one available, create your own). There should be equal spacing between each player. For organizational purposes, create 3 groups. Number each player 1, 2, or 3 (should be an equal number of each). Have the group of 1s come to the middle of the circle with a ball each; the 2s and 3s are on the outside. Once the game gets going, a player in the middle will pass the ball to a player on the outside (and then follows his pass), who then knocks the ball sideways to a player on his immediate left or right. At this point, the receiver touches the ball in the direction it just came from, while the person who passed the ball runs around him (overlap). As the overlapping player rounds the player with the ball, that player releases it into space in the circle and the cycle repeats itself. Work in intervals of 30-45 seconds, it will take a few explanations and some trial and error, but this is the most powerful way to teach an overlap in context. (The passes are numbered and the run is outlined to make it easier to understand).

Possible Progressions:

- Mandate the sideways pass must go in a certain direction (e.g. you must pass the ball to the person on your right).
- Mandate that the sideways pass must be first time.
- Mandate that players must communicate (e.g., hold, release).
- Mandate that when a player is released into the middle following an overlap, he must immediately do a "move" on the ball (e.g. Cruyff turn, Maradona, etc.).

Activity #1: The Nickens Plus One

Time: Approximately 15 minutes.

Area: Square grid of about 12 x 12 yards (W x L). You can make your grid(s) smaller or bigger depending on how many players you have and their ability levels.

Activity: This game works best when you have different color cones, but it works just fine if you don't. Two teams line up diagonally opposite from each other (per the diagram above). One team has the balls. There is a neutral player in each grid (he stays in for duration of the round). The player with the ball plays into the neutral and then he and his partner make overlapping runs to try and get a goal by dribbling the ball through the gate. If the defender steals the ball, he can then try to counter attack and dribble through one of her offensive gates (see diagram - blue gates). Go for 60-90 seconds (keeping score) and then swap roles. Whichever team scores the most goals, wins. Neutral players CAN score – which encourages the defenders to defend him. This is a good activity to see how players solve offensive problems in tight spaces.

Possible Progressions:

- Double points for a goal that comes directly from an overlap.
- Make the gates bigger/smaller.
- Make the grid bigger/smaller.

Activity #2: 2v1 Continuous*Overlap

Time: Approximately 20 minutes.

Area: If you have a marked 18-yard box, use it and then mark out another one with cones to create a 36 x 44 yard (L x W) playing grid.

Activity: Divide the players into 2 even teams. Have them line up as shown in the diagram above. The balls should be divided equally and diagonally (per the diagram). To begin, you can play the ball into the middle. Players go to the other line once they have had their turn (e.g., attacker goes to the winger line and vice versa). Any time the ball crosses a line (side, end, goal), the team whose possession it would be restarts the game from their side with a new pair of players (the defending pair stays in). Also, any time a ball crosses the end line from a shot (including a goal), the shooter must run around the corner while the 2 defenders drop out (the attacking team now becomes the numbers down defending team), and a new attack begins by 2 forwards to make it 2v1 (with the recovering defender who just shot the ball running around the corner). Play first team to a set number of goals (e.g., 5, 7, 9) and give the losing team a consequence. After the consequence, you can ask the guided discovery questions, while the players catch their breath.

The idea is for the player with the ball to pass it as quickly as possible to the winger who then takes it inside, thus creating an overlapping angle. After that, the best choice depends on what the defenders do.

Possible Progressions:

- Give 2 points for goals that result from overlaps.
- Put all players on a touch restriction (e.g., 3 touches).
- All goals must be first time finishes.

Activity #3: 3v2 Continuous*Overlap

Time: Approximately 20 minutes.

Area: If you have a marked 18-yard box, use it and then mark out another one with cones to create a 36 x 44 yard (L x W) playing grid.

Activity: This activity is a progression from the previous one. By adding another player to each team, you have made the game more complex and therefore more difficult to execute an overlap. The player starting with the ball may choose to play directly to the wide player (as shown in the diagram), or he may choose to play a square pass and look to overlap on the opposite wing. If you see someone attempt an overlap in this game, celebrate it because overlaps are rarely seen in youth soccer. This is your opportunity to change that!

Possible Progressions:

- Give 2 points for goals that result from overlaps.
- Put all players on a touch restriction (e.g., 3 touches).
- All goals must be first time finishes.

End of Practice Scrimmage: Half Field Scrimmage

Time: Approximately 30 minutes (or whatever is left of practice).

Area: One half of the field (playing to one big goal). By putting a Coerver goal on the halfway line, you can have two of these scrimmages at the same time. Depending on your numbers, you may want to play the entire width of the field or just the width of the 18-yard box. Typically, I will play the width of the 18 for 5v5 - 7v7; however, if you find that space too restrictive, you can always open it up.

Activity: Play even numbers and arrange teams in a formation that reflects your desired game day formation. This is a good game to play if you have the space and the numbers. If you don't, no need to worry, just divide up the players into two even teams and let them play in the space you do have available.

Possible Progressions:

- Allow double the points for goals scored immediately following an overlap.
- Add a neutral(s) to give the team in possession an advantage.
- Put one or both teams on touch restrictions (e.g., 3 touch max, 2 touch max).

Session #11: Short, Short Long

This session is not for players new to the game of soccer. "Short, short, long" (or SSL) describes the sequence of passes and usually involves at least three players. It is designed to break through defensive units and is particularly useful for springing an offside trap. Your players need to be skilled enough to execute the passes, but also possess the cognitive abilities to "see" the future, as SSL involves playing a ball into space into the path of a player making an appropriately timed run. Some coaches call this combination play "Up, Back, and Through," which is equally appropriate.

What will players learn from this session?

- Three of more players work together to beat the defense and accomplish their objective (attacking mindset).
- Players will learn how to most effectively utilize SSL (attacking mindset, support, penetration).
- This activity encourages players to develop spatial awareness and move accordingly in order to help their team maintain possession of the ball before finding the penetrating pass (support, mobility width, depth).
- It also encourages players to switch the point of the attack to a less well-defended area and to play in tight spaces where necessary (width and improvisation).
- Players will be able to spot "triggers" for when a SSL is going to do the most damage (attacking mindset, penetration).

Coaching Points for the session:

- As the first pass going forward is very important to set this play up, praise players who have the courage to play a short pass forward and then look to receive it back.
- Praise players when they create space for themselves by taking a defender away and then checking for the ball with a change of pace and direction.
- Praise players who set the ball back ready to be struck first time on the receiving player's dominant foot (if there is the opportunity to do so).
- Praise players when they make appropriate decisions about when and where to attempt a SSL (not the execution/outcome).
- Praise creativity in the face of a problem (even when it doesn't come off).
- Praise "runners" when they make angled runs into space (slashing runs) that are difficult to defend against (as opposed to straight runs that often get the player caught offside, unless

he is starting from a position between the other team's defense and midfield).

Guided discovery questions for the session: (can be asked at any point)

- What are the situations when the SSL is "on"? Why?
- As the person playing the first pass, what type of pass should you give? Why?
- As the player "setting" the ball, what type of pass should you give? Why?
- As the player hitting the "long" or penetrating pass, where should you look to play it? Why?
- As the "runner," how do you know when to make your run into space?
- As the "runner," what type of run(s) should you make? Why?

Warm-up Activity: 5v2

Time: Approximately 15 minutes.

Area: Set up grids of approximately 10 x 10 yards (make bigger if you have weaker players).

Activity: While staying in the grid at all times, 5 players attempt to keep the ball away from 2. Play rounds of 30-45 seconds. When the time is up, change the pair in the middle. Have each group keep count of the highest number of consecutive passes they managed. The first pass is always "free" (e.g., the defenders must allow it). If you feel it is appropriate, have the group with the lowest number of passes do a quick consequence (e.g., one from: 5 knees to chest, 5 pushups, 5 sit-ups, etc.). The pair of defenders with the most passes against them does the consequence, too. If your players are struggling in having 2 defenders to play against, start with 1 defender. Once they get proficient (e.g., can make 5 passes in a row a few times - review some of the guided discovery questions), add the second defender back in. You can also make the grid bigger - this means more space for the defender(s) to cover, which is always in the attacking team's favor!

5v2 is a great warm-up activity for your team. It gets them a lot of touches on the ball, requires them to deal with pressure, and forces them to make decisions. Depending on numbers, you can make it 4v2, 4v1, or 3v1.

Possible Progressions:

- Put touch restrictions on the players (e.g., 3 touch max, then 2 touch max, then 1 touch).
- Play 2 touch max, but mandate that after a player has two touches the following player to receive the ball must play it first time (there can be unlimited 1 touch passes, but as soon as someone takes 2 touches, the next player must play it first time).
- Mandate that players must follow their pass (constant movement/chaos).

Activity #1: Over the River

Time: Approximately 15 minutes.

Area: 15 x 40 yards divided into a 15 x 15 box, a 15 x 10 box, then another 15 x 15 box (W x L).

Activity: Split your players up into 3 teams of 5 (works with teams of 4, too). Put 2 teams in each of the 15x15 boxes and the remaining team in the middle zone. The coach stands off to one side with the balls. He serves a ball into one of the end zones. As soon as he does, the team in the middle zone can send 2 defenders into that zone (essentially 5v2). If the team in possession makes 5 consecutive passes, they can attempt to send the ball "over the river" to the other end zone, at which point (if they are successful) 2 new players from the middle zone will go to play 5v2. If the defending team wins the ball (or intercepts it in the middle zone), they swap with the other team. Play first team to score 3 points. Mix up the teams as necessary. I will often try and put players in their positions (e.g., a center forward with a couple of center midfielders and wide midfielders, or a center midfielder with two center defenders and wide defenders). If your players are struggling to string 5 consecutive passes together, lower the target to 4, or 3. Once they find success, then you can get back up to 5 passes. Another trick is to make the field wider (whenever you do this, it means the defenders have to work harder, which makes it more likely for the attacking team to get their passes in).

Possible Progressions:

- Increase the number of passes required before attempting to go "over the river" (e.g., from 5 to 6, 6 to 7 – doing so in small increments will help the players find success).
- Put touch restrictions on the players (e.g., 3 touch max, then 2 touch max, then 1 touch).
- Mandate that the ball must go "over the river" first time.

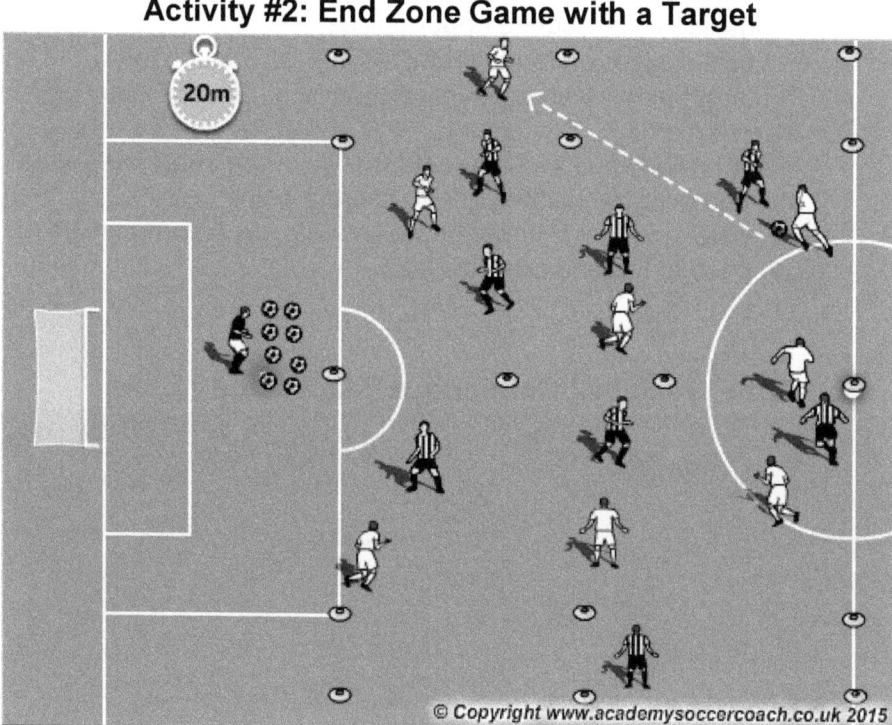

Activity #2: End Zone Game with a Target

Time: Approximately 20 minutes.

Area: 40 x 50 yards (W x L) inclusive of a 5-yard deep end zone at each end. Depending on your numbers and available space, make the field as big as you can (use existing field lines to help).

Activity: Divide up the players into two even teams. The coach should keep the balls off to one side (around midfield). Teams score a point when they pass the ball into their end zone player and (s)he successfully passes the ball out to another teammate. The player that passed the ball into the target replaces him/her and the former target player follows his/her pass and is now in the middle (this keeps all players as active as possible). Defenders are not allowed in the end zones. Play first team to score 3-5 points, then ask guided discovery questions as appropriate. Repeat as necessary.

Regressions: If your players are struggling to get the ball into the end zone player, allow balls to be served in the air and the target to use her hands (which should reduce the margin for error and therefore make it easier to be successful). When the target player receives it, she can roll it out to a teammate and the game may continue.

Possible Progressions:

- Add a neutral(s), so the attacking team is always numbers up (producing more scoring opportunities).
- Put field players on touch restrictions (e.g., 3 touch max).
- Put target players on touch restriction (e.g., 2 touch max, then 1 touch max).
- Add a halfway line and mandate that all of the attacking team must be over the halfway line to score a point.
- Mandate a certain number of passes (e.g., 5) before players can pass to the end zone target.

Activity #3: 3v2 Continuous*Stacked and Level

Time: Approximately 20 minutes.

Area: If you have a marked 18-yard box, use it and then mark out another one with cones to create a 36 x 44 yard (L x W) playing grid.

Activity: Divide the players into 2 even teams. Have them line up as shown in the diagram above. The balls should be divided equally and diagonally (per the diagram). To begin, you can play the ball into the middle. Where appropriate, players go to the other line once they have had their turn (e.g., attacker goes to the other attacker line). Any time the ball crosses a line (side, end, goal), the team whose possession it would be restarts the game from their side with a new pair of players (the defending pair stays in). Also, any time a ball crosses the end line from a shot (including a goal), the shooter must run around the corner while the 3 defenders drop out (the attacking team now becomes the numbers down defending team), and a new attack begins by 3 forwards to make it 3v2 (with the recovering defender who just shot the ball running around the corner). Play first team to a set number of goals (e.g., 5, 7, 9) and give the losing team a consequence (could be resetting the balls). After the consequence, you can ask the guided discovery questions, while the players catch their breath.

Like the other "Continuous" games, this one will take a few rounds for the players to understand. Again, be consistent with the rules, and highlight the situations where players have found success in playing up to and off the target (or "stacked") player.

Possible Progressions:

- Give 2 points for goals resulting from a SSL (up to the checking forward, back to the original passer, and then through to the third player running).
- Give 3 points for goals resulting from a SSL that is all one touch play (the passes and the shot).

End of Practice Scrimmage:
Half Field Scrimmage with Bumpers

Time: Approximately 30 minutes (or whatever is left of practice).

Area: One half of the field (playing to one big goal). By putting a Coerver goal on the halfway line, you can have two of these scrimmages at the same time. Depending on your numbers, you may want to play the entire width of the field or just the width of the 18-yard box. Typically, I will play the width of the 18 for 5v5 - 7v7; however, if you find that space too restrictive, you can always open it up.

Activity: Put "bumper" players on each sideline and diagonally on the end line (as per the diagram). Bumpers have one touch. Having bumpers incentivizes your players to look up and try to play the ball forward or wide as early as possible. Play even numbers and arrange teams in a formation that reflects your desired game day formation.

Possible Progressions:

- Allow double the points for goals involving a SSL in the build up.
- Add a neutral(s) to give the team in possession an advantage.
- Put one or both teams on touch restrictions (e.g., 3 touch max, 2 touch max).

Session #12: Switching the Point of the Attack

Switching the point of the attack is an essential strategy in youth soccer because very often you will see most of the players on the pitch condensed in one sector of the field (some people refer to this as the "beehive"). Moving the ball from a highly congested area of the field and getting it to an open player in a different part of the field is a lot easier said than done! As such, this session is designed to get your players thinking about the open spaces on the field, why it is important to have depth to an attack, and the best ways of getting the ball away from pressure.

What will players learn from this session?

- Successful players keep their heads up and eyes open to see where the space is, but also to recognize the visual cues of the defender(s) (e.g., have the defenders been "dragged" over to the ball, leaving the weak side unguarded?)
- Successful players, especially the ones who are not the quickest, will look to disguise their movements (improvisation) by perhaps playing a first time ball to the weak side, or by pretending to play in one direction and then going in the opposite one.
- This session encourages players to develop spatial awareness and move accordingly in order to help their team maintain possession of the ball (support, mobility width, depth).
- It will also encourage players to switch the point of the attack to a less well-defended area and to play in tight spaces where necessary (width and improvisation).

Coaching points for the session:

- Praise players when they make an angle and space in order to relieve pressure when a teammate has possession in a tight space.
- Praise players who get their head up to see what options are available before making the pass.
- Praise players who move the ball from a congested area to a less congested area of the field.
- Praise creativity (even when it doesn't come off).
- Praise players when they disguise their intentions.
- Praise players for their pass selection (e.g. lofted, driven, side foot, outside of the foot) in order to switch the point of the attack.

- Praise a player who receives the ball on their "weak side" and then takes his first touch to immediately penetrate space.

Guided discovery questions for the session: (can be asked at any point)

- Do you want to make the field bigger or smaller when you have the ball? How can you do this? Why should you do this?
- What is the first question you should ask yourself when you have the ball?
- What type of support can you provide to give the person on the ball options to get the ball out to the weak side (less well defended side)?
- When transferring the ball from a congested area to a less congested area, should you play slow or fast? Why?
- What else can you do in this game to be successful? Explain that to me.

Warm-up Activity: The Circle Game With Pressure

Time: Approximately 20 minutes.

Activity: This activity is a progression from the previous one, which will allow you to give your players a quick water break and then get straight back into action. This time, create 3 groups. Number each player 1, 2, or 3. Have the group of 1s come to the middle of the circle; the 2s and 3s are on the outside. The 2s should have a ball at their feet, while the 3s should be "open." This situation (where the 2s have the balls and the 3s don't) is only to get the activity started. Once the game gets going, there are simply players in the middle receiving and passing and players on the outside who are passing and receiving. Working in intervals of 30-45 seconds, the outside players pass the ball to players in the middle whose job is to pass it back to a different person. Have the inside players keep count of their completed passes. If you feel it is appropriate, have the person with the fewest passes do a quick consequence on the outside of the circle.

Possible Progressions:
- Mandate that the players on the inside use a certain foot (e.g., only right, then only left, then either foot).
- Every player must take two touches (mandate a certain surface to control the ball; e.g., only the outside of the foot, only the inside, only the sole, etc.).
- Take away a ball (creates competition in the middle for a ball; leads to receiving under pressure).
- Take away another ball (intensifies the above).
- Have outside players serve the ball from their hands in the air (e.g., knee height, chest height, bouncing ball).

Activity #1: Target Ball

Time: Approximately 20 minutes.

Area: 40 x 50 yards (W x L) - make as big as possible! In the diagram above, I make use of existing lines.

Activity: Put a cone in each corner of the field, then 2 or 3 others (equally distributed) along each end line (see diagram). Balance a ball on top of each cone on the end line. Divide players into 2 teams. The objective is to successfully knock a ball off the cone (with the game ball). Team A defends their side and attempts to score on the other end (vice versa for Team B). If a player shoots and misses, (s)he must run to retrieve the ball, while the defending team can take the ball off the cone that the attacker missed (meaning that they will be temporarily "numbers up"). Play first team to 3 goals, then review the guided discovery questions and move through progressions. If defenders are just standing by cones, say that 5 consecutive passes equals a goal. This should entice the defending team to come out and play.

Depending on your numbers (e.g., if you have 16 or more), you may want to go for two smaller fields in order to maximize players' touches on the ball and exposure to learning situations. It is good to experiment and see what works best for your group.

Possible Progressions:

- Play transition (whereby once a team scores at one end, they then immediately go and try and score at the other end).
- Add a halfway line and mandate that to score, all of the attacking team's players must be in the attacking half.
- Add a neutral(s), so that the attacking team is always at an advantage.
- Put all players on a touch restriction (e.g., 3 touch maximum).
- Finally, mandate that "goals" must be first time (e.g., players must knock the ball off the cone with their first touch!).

Activity #2: The 6 Small Goal Game

Time: 10-15 minutes.

Area: 40 x 50 yards (W x L). Depending on your numbers and available space, make the field as big as you can (use existing field lines to help).

Activity: Make 6 cone goals (one in each corner of the field and one in the center at each end). Goals should be approximately 4-6 yards wide (bigger goals = greater opportunities for success). Let teams play against each other - even numbers. No goalkeepers. This game encourages players to start thinking about the "weak side" and to switch the ball out of pressure.

Possible Progressions:

- Put in a halfway line and mandate that all attacking players must be in the attacking half for a goal to count (this discourages goaltending/hanging back).
- Add a neutral(s) to ensure the attacking team is always numbers up.
- Play transition (whereby when Team A scores in one goal, they are now trying to score in the opposite goal - Team B also switches).

- Put touch restrictions on the players (e.g., 3 touch max, then 2 touch, 1 touch) whereby if someone takes too many touches, it results in a direct free kick to the other team.
- Play 3 touch max, but to score it must be 1 touch ("first time finish").

Activity #3: 3v2 Continuous*Stacked and Wide* Ball Starts Wide

Time: Approximately 20 minutes.

Area: If you have a marked 18-yard box, use it and then mark out another one with cones to create a 36 x 44 yard (L x W) playing grid.

Activity: Divide the players into 2 even teams. Have them line up as shown in the diagram above. The balls should be divided equally and diagonally (per the diagram). To begin, you can play the ball into the middle. End line players go to the other line once they have had their turn, while side players return to their line (e.g., attacker goes to a different attack line – I would suggest a clockwise rotation). Any time the ball crosses a line (side, end, goal), the team whose possession it would be restarts the game from their side with a new pair (the defending pair stays in). Also, any time a ball crosses the end line from a shot (including a goal), the shooter must run around the corner while the 3 defenders drop out (the attacking team now becomes the numbers down defending team), and a new attack begins with 3 forwards to make it 3v2 (with the recovering defender who just shot the ball running around the corner). Play first team to a set number of goals (e.g., 5, 7, 9) and give the losing team a consequence (e.g., resetting the balls). After the consequence, you can ask the guided discovery questions, while the players catch their breath.

Possible Progressions:

- Give 2 points for first time finishes (encourages combination plays, crosses, etc.).
- Put all players on a touch restriction (e.g., 3 touch maximum).

End of Practice Scrimmage: Full Field Scrimmage

Time: Approximately 30 minutes (or whatever is left of practice).

Area: Using a marked field, use the entire space! If you don't have a marked field, make your field as big as you can.

Activity: Play even numbers and arrange teams in a formation that reflects your desired game day formation. This is a good game to play if you have the space and the numbers. If you don't, not to worry, just divide up the players into two even teams and let them play in the space you do have available. By playing the full field, there will be lots of space which should allow for easier switches to open players.

Possible Progressions:
- Allow double the points for goals scored immediately following a "switch."
- Add a neutral(s) to give the team in possession an advantage, but define the zone in which that player(s) can operate (e.g. in the middle of the field, so they are always an option to switch the point of the attack).
- Put one or both teams on touch restrictions (e.g., 3 touch max, 2 touch max).

Session #13: Introduction to Converting from Crosses

Converting from crosses is an important, yet often neglected, aspect of attacking play in soccer. At the youth level particularly, players will make straight runs into the penalty box, arrive far too early and then stand almost on the goal line. Similarly, teams that have not practiced crossing will often struggle against defenses that employ a low block (deep lying) strategy that is compact and forces the play out wide. This session will give your players a sense of purpose and confidence when the ball goes wide in the attacking third. It is appropriate for moderately experienced players and above, but can be modified as needed.

What will players learn from this session?

- Players work together to beat the defense and accomplish their objective (attacking mindset).
- Predetermined patterns of play don't always work well because defenders don't always do what we want them to do! As such, attackers are encouraged to figure out "what works best" when the ball is in wide positions (attacking mindset and penetration).
- The supporting attacker(s) must offer effective angles of support and get into good shooting positions (support, width, and mobility).
- Because the ball is served from a wide position into the box, the forwards must figure out the best angles of support/"runs" and come up with creative finishing solutions in order to score goals (improvisation, support).

Coaching Points for the session:

- When appropriate, praise players for holding their runs and then sprinting to the near post (so they arrive at the near post as the ball would).
- Praise creativity (even when it doesn't come off).
- Praise players when they disguise their intentions.
- Praise players who create space for themselves and/or their teammates with clever runs and touches.
- Praise players who make good decisions when shooting (e.g. take a touch when there is time, use their side foot when placement is needed, stooping to head a ball that is at an awkward height).

Guided discovery questions for the session: (can be asked at any point)

- How can you "draw the defender in"? Show me.

- When you pass the ball to your partner, what is the best type of pass and why?
- Where should the winger (person starting with the ball) take their first touch? Why?
- Where do you want to "cross" the ball? At what speed/height? With which surface of the foot should you use? Why?
- What type of run should you make if you see a space at the near post? Why? How?
- How can you finish the ball accurately most of the time in that situation? Why?

Warm-up Activity: Flying Wingers

Time: Approximately 10 minutes.

Area: In front of a big goal.

Activity: Set up four groups of players as per the diagram. Players in the middle take it in turns passing the ball out wide. In the example, the central player with the ball is passing the ball wide left (next time, the central player on the other side will pass the ball wide right). The winger then takes a touch or two towards the end line and will cross the ball for the two central players who have made back post and near post runs, respectively. Players return to their same line. Play rounds of 2 minutes and then switch the wingers.

Possible Progressions:

- Set a target of 10 goals in 2 minutes.
- Award double points for first time finishes.
- Put the wingers on a touch restriction (e.g., 2 touch maximum).

Activity #1: The Crossing Game*Progression #1

Time: Approximately 15 minutes.

Area: 50 x 30 yards (W x L)

Activity: Set up a cone on the angle of the six-yard box and end line on both sides (these will be the starting points for your defenders). Set up a cone on each side of the field about 5 yards in from the sideline and about 30 yards from the goal line (these will be the starting points for your crossers). Set up 2 cones about 12 yards back from the 18-yard box, centered, and with approximately 10 yards between them (these will be the starting points for the forwards). Finally, set up 2 cones 5 yards behind the last set of cones (this is where extra players will wait). Assign 6 defenders and a goalkeeper. Two defenders stand behind each cone, level with the goal line. The balls should be evenly split up and at the wide positions.

Upon the coach's' signal, one of the wide players dribbles the ball toward the goal. When she takes her first touch, the defender on her side comes out to defend her; meanwhile the 2 forwards are also in play and they play 3v1 to goal. When the ball goes out of bounds, the crosser goes to the forward line, while one of the forwards goes to the crosser line. The forward who remains a forward goes to the back of the other forward line. As soon as the ball goes out of play, the coach signals for play to begin from the other side of the field.

Progression #1: Once your attacking teams have started to understand the game and are regularly creating scoring opportunities, then it is time to add the second defender. Now, the early pass to the middle is not such an easy option because there is another defender to guard the space. Depending on your numbers, you can add another 2 players to the defending team (with 1 defender coming from each side).

Activity #2: The Crossing Game*Progression #2

Time: Approximately 15-20 minutes.

Activity: Set up a cone on the angle of the six-yard box and end line on both sides (these will be the starting points for your defenders). Set up a cone on each side of the field about 5 yards in from the sideline and about 30 yards from the goal line (these will be the starting points for your crossers). Set up 2 cones about 12 yards back from the 18-yard box, centered, and with approximately 10 yards between them (these will be the starting points for the forwards). Finally, set up 2 cones, 5 yards behind the last set of cones (this is where extra players will wait). Assign 6 defenders and a goalkeeper. Two defenders stand behind each cone, level with the goal line. The balls should be evenly split up and at the wide positions.

Upon the coach's signal, one of the wide players dribbles the ball toward the goal. When she takes her first touch, the defender on her side comes out to defend her; meanwhile the 2 forwards are also in play and they play 3v1 to goal. When the ball goes out of bounds, the crosser goes to the forward line, while one of the forwards goes to the crosser line. The forward who remains a forward goes to the back of the other forward line. As soon as the ball goes out of play, the coach signals for play to begin from the other side of the field.

Progression #2: Have the winger on the opposite side of the field join in the attack, making it a 4v2 situation. Play rounds of 90-120 seconds.

Activity #3: 2v1 Continuous*Wide*Ball Passed in

Time: Approximately 20 minutes.

Area: If you have a marked 18-yard box, use it and then mark out another one with cones to create a 36 x 44 yard (L x W) playing grid.

Activity: Divide the players into 2 even teams. Have them line up as shown in the diagram above. The balls should be divided equally and diagonally (per the diagram). To begin, you can play the ball into the middle. Players go to the other line once they have had their turn (e.g., attacker goes to the other attacker line). Any time the ball crosses a line (side, end, goal) the team whose possession it would be restarts the game from their side with a new pair (the defending pair stays in). Also, any time a ball crosses the end line from a shot (including a goal), the shooter must run around the corner while the 2 defenders drop out (the attacking team now becomes the numbers down defending team), and a new attack begins by 2 forwards to make it 2v1 (with the recovering defender who just shot the ball running around the corner). Play first team to a set number of goals (e.g., 5, 7, 9) and give the losing team a consequence. After the consequence, you can ask the guided discovery questions, while the players catch their breath.

All restarts must begin with a pass to the wide player.

Possible Progressions:

- Move the balls to the other side (move the players, too, so the wide player is always on the "weak side").
- Give 2 points for goals resulting directly from crosses.
- Give 3 points for first time finishes (encourages quality crosses).

End of Practice Scrimmage: 18s Extended Out

Time: Approximately 30 minutes (or whatever is left of practice).

Area: As per the diagram, extend the 18-yard box out to the sidelines.

Activity: Play even numbers and arrange teams in a formation that reflects your desired game day formation. The field dimensions makes for a shorter, but wider playing area – perfect for working on crossing and finishing because it means there is more space in wide areas.

Progressions:

- Award double points for goals that come from crosses.
- Award triple points for first time finishes from crosses.
- Award quadruple points for finishes that result from an overlap and cross.

Session #14: Introduction to Using a Target Player

All teams have target players that are used as the "go to" players. Usually this player will be a forward and serve as the fulcrum for attacks (e.g. the ball gets played into him and he holds it up, before laying it off to oncoming midfielders). Target players can also play as the "number 10" (finding space between the opposition's defensive and midfield lines) or as the deep lying central midfielder who looks to get the ball from the defense and then turn and launch attacks. This session will help the target players understand their roles and also expose the team to the idea of how to best utilize a target player.

What will players learn from this session?

- Players work together to beat the defense and accomplish their objective around an attacking focal point (attacking mindset).
- Movement is essential to opening up passing channels in order for the target player to receive the ball (support, mobility).
- The types of forward passes that are most successful in order to set up goal scoring opportunities (ways of penetration, attacking mindset).
- What to do when the ball goes into the target player (support, mobility).

Coaching Points for the session:

- Praise target players when they create a better angle for a forward pass (it may only be a step sideways – it doesn't always have to be a "run").
- Praise players when they make appropriate decisions about when and where to try to play the ball forward to the target player (not the execution/outcome).
- Praise creativity (even when it doesn't come off).
- Praise players when they disguise their intentions.
- Praise players when they make runs to receive the ball as the ball is played into the target player.

Guided discovery questions for the session: (can be asked at any point)

- When should you look to play the ball forward to the target player? Why?
- What type of pass should you look to play forwards to the target player? Why?

- What support can you provide when the ball goes into the target player? Which run(s) will be most dangerous and potentially lead to goal-scoring opportunities? Why?
- [Target player] How can you provide an angle for the ball to make it as easy as possible for the passer to get the ball to your feet as close to the opposition's goal as possible? Show me. Why?
- When you receive the ball, where should you look to take your first touch in order to create a better potential goal-scoring opportunity for a teammate within two passes? Why?
- What opportunities are there when the target player checks in for the ball and brings a defender with him? Why? How can you exploit this?
- What else can you do in this game to be successful? Explain that to me.

Warm-up Activity: The Circle Game With Defensive Pressure

Time: Approximately 20 minutes.

Activity: Create two groups of players (1s and 2s). Have the group of 1s come to the middle of the circle; the 2s are on the outside and have a ball at their feet. Choose 2 or 3 of the 1s to be defenders. Working in intervals of 30-45 seconds, the outside players pass the ball to the attackers in the middle whose job is to pass it back taking as few touches as possible. The defenders are simply trying to disrupt play and can defend as much as they like. Make sure everyone gets a turn(s) at being a defender.

Possible Progressions:

- Mandate that players must pass the ball back to a different outside player (need to reduce the number of players with balls to make this work).
- Put inside players on a touch restriction (e.g. 3 touch maximum).

Activity #1: End Zone Game with a Target Under Pressure

Time: Approximately 20 minutes.

Area: 40 x 50 yards (W x L) inclusive of a 5-10 yard deep end zone at each end. Depending on your numbers and available space, make the field as big as you can (use existing field lines to help).

Activity: Divide up the players into two even teams. The coach should keep the balls off to one side (around midfield). Teams score a point when they pass the ball into their end zone player and (s)he successfully passes the ball out to another teammate. The player that passed the ball into the target replaces him/her and the former target player follows his/her pass and is now in the middle (this keeps all players as active as possible). Each team has a player in each end zone; therefore, there should be pressure as soon as the ball enters the zone. Play first team to score 3-5 points, then ask guided discovery questions as appropriate. Repeat as necessary.

Possible Progressions:

- Add a neutral(s), so the attacking team is always numbers up (producing more scoring opportunities).
- Put field players on touch restrictions (e.g., 3 touch max).
- Put target players on touch restriction (e.g., 2 touch max, then 1 touch max).

Activity #2: 6v6 Plus 2 Targets

Time: Approximately 20 minutes.

Area: If you have a marked 18-yard box, use it and then mark out another one with cones to create a 36 x 44 yards (L x W) playing grid.

Activity: This game works best with 18 players (2 goalkeepers and 16 outfield players), but can easily be modified to fit your numbers). Divide the players into 3 even (ability) teams with a goalkeeper in each goal. The balls should be divided evenly and placed in each goal for quick and easy retrieval by the goalkeeper. Each team picks two players to serve as offensive targets/bumpers. These targets/bumpers have 1 touch, and can move sideways but may not come onto the field of play. There are no offsides in this game. Play first team to a set number of goals (e.g., 2, 3) and then switch the targets/bumpers.

Possible Progressions:

- Give 2 points for each goal that comes directly from a "bumper" player.
- Put all players inside the grid on a touch restriction (e.g., 2 touch maximum).
- Mandate that all goals must be a first time finish.

Activity #3: 3v2 Continuous*Double Stacked

Time: Approximately 20 minutes.

Area: If you have a marked 18-yard box, use it and then mark out another one with cones to create a 36 x 44 yard (L x W) playing grid.

Activity: Divide the players into 2 even teams. Have them line up as shown in the diagram above. The balls should be divided equally and diagonally (per the diagram). To begin, you can play the ball into the middle. Where appropriate, players go to the other line once they have had their turn (e.g., attacker goes to the other attacker line). Any time the ball crosses a line (side, end, goal), the team whose possession it would be restarts the game from their side with a new pair (the defending pair stays in). Also, any time a ball crosses the end line from a shot (including a goal), the shooter must run around the corner while the 3 defenders drop out (the attacking team now becomes the numbers down defending team), and a new attack begins by 3 forwards to make it 3v2 (with the recovering defender who just shot the ball running around the corner). Play first team to a set number of goals (e.g., 5, 7, 9) and give the losing team a consequence (e.g., resetting balls). After the consequence, you can ask the guided discovery questions, while the players catch their breath.

Possible Progressions:

- Give 2 points for combinations that involve the use of a target player setting up a goal (ball goes up and comes back).
- Give 3 points for a combination that involves the target player laying the ball back first time with the goal also being scored from a first time (one touch) shot.

End of Practice Scrimmage: Hit the Targets!

Time: Approximately 30 minutes (or whatever is left of practice).

Area: Using a marked field, make an 18-yard box with cones (using the halfway line as the edge of the box). If you don't have a marked field, make your field as big as you can (but not as long as a game field).

Activity: Each team picks two players to serve as offensive targets/bumpers. These targets/bumpers have 1 touch, and can move sideways but may not come onto the field of play. There are no offsides in this game. Play first team to a set number of goals (e.g., 2, 3) and then switch the targets/bumpers.

By reducing the length of the field, you can get more action by the goal and the players won't get as tired as they would from a full field scrimmage, yet there is still plenty of space in which the players can operate.

Possible Progressions:

- Give 2 points for each goal that comes directly from a "bumper" player.
- Put all players inside the grid on a touch restriction (e.g., 2 touch maximum).
- Mandate that all goals must be a first time finish.

Session #15: Introduction to Getting Numbers in the Attack

Your team will not score many goals if you do not get numbers (players) into the attack. Many teams, especially at the younger youth levels will rely on one or two players who might be bigger, faster, stronger, and/or more skilled than the rest of the team, to score goals. Although this strategy may benefit your team in the short term, you are neglecting the potential of your other players to learn/contribute in the medium/long term. Also, when you come up against a team with players that can shut down your "horses" you will most likely struggle. This session is designed to teach your players that when your team has the ball, they are ALL part of the offense, and they might be required to get forward to support the attack.

What will players learn from this session?

- Players work together to beat the defense and accomplish their objective (attacking mindset).
- Players constantly change pace and direction with the ball in a confined space (mobility).
- Players will learn where, when, and how to most effectively spring the overlap (attacking mindset, support, penetration).
- Players will learn how to use the overlap as a decoy to create space/a scoring opportunity (improvisation, attacking mindset).
- Successful players, especially the ones who are not the fastest, will look to disguise their movements (improvisation).
- Successful players keep their heads up and eyes open to see where the space is, but also to recognize the visual cues of the defender(s) (e.g., where is she looking, are they favoring one particular side, are they weak on one side, what is their body position?).

Coaching Points for the session:

- Praise players when they create a better angle for an overlap by taking their first touch in the direction they received the ball from.
- Praise players who change speed and direction to attempt an overlap.
- Praise players when they make appropriate decisions about when and where to try an overlap (not the execution/outcome).
- Praise creativity (even when it doesn't come off).
- Praise players when they disguise their intentions.
- Praise players when they use the overlap as a decoy.

- Praise players who create space for themselves and/or their teammates with clever runs.

Guided discovery questions for the session: (can be asked at any point)

- How can you "draw the defender in"? Show me.
- When you pass the ball to your partner, what is the best type of pass and why?
- When you receive the ball, where should you look to take your first touch in order to create a better angle for an overlap? Why? Show me.
- When making the overlapping run, is it easier to beat the defender when you go slow or fast? Why?

Warm-up Activity: 5v2*Outside

Time: Approximately 10-15 minutes.

Area: Set up grids of approximately 10 x 10 yards (make bigger if you have weaker players).

Activity: Standing outside the grid, 5 players attempt to keep the ball away from 2. Play rounds of 30-45 seconds. When the time is up, change the pair in the middle. Have each group keep count of the highest number of consecutive passes they managed. The first pass is always "free" (e.g., the defenders must allow it). The ball must always cross two lines to be considered a complete pass.

Possible Progressions:

- Put touch restrictions on the players (e.g., 3 touch max, then 2 touch max, then 1 touch).
- Play 2 touch max, but mandate that after a player has two touches the following player to receive the ball must play it first time (there can be unlimited 1 touch passes, but as soon as someone takes 2 touches, the next player must play it first time).
- Mandate that players must follow their pass (constant movement/chaos).

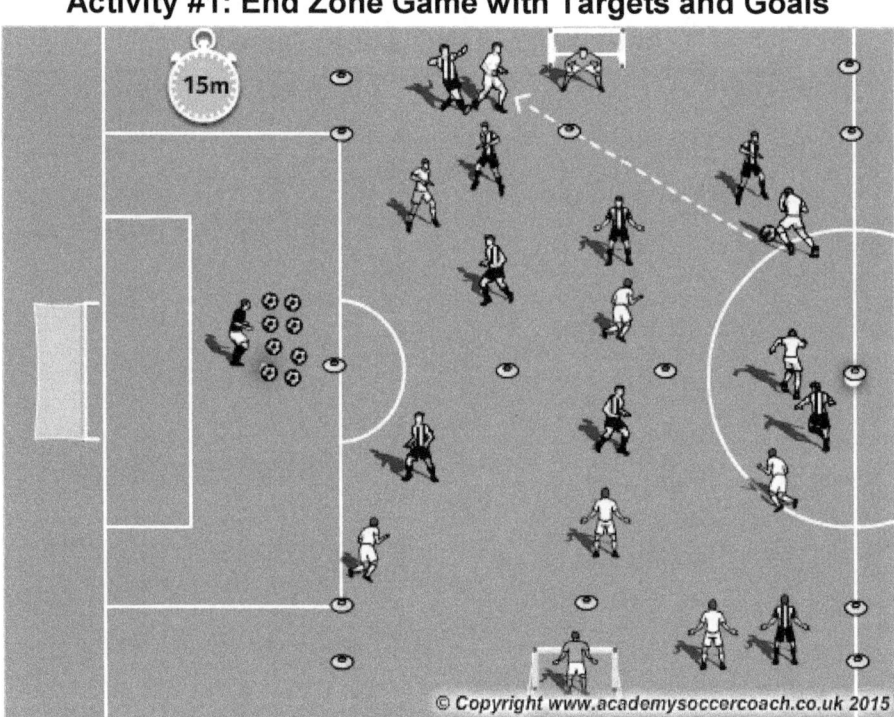

Activity #1: End Zone Game with Targets and Goals

Time: Approximately 15 minutes.

Area: 40 x 50 yards (W x L) inclusive of a 5-10 yard deep end zone at each end. Depending on your numbers and available space, make the field as big as you can (use existing field lines to help).

Activity: Divide the players into two even teams. The coach should keep the balls off to one side (around midfield). Teams score double points when they pass the ball into their end zone player and he successfully passes the ball out to another teammate within 2 touches (or shoots and scores himself). Each team has a player in each end zone; therefore, there should be pressure as soon as the ball enters the zone. Play first team to score 3-5 points, then ask guided discovery questions as appropriate. Repeat as necessary.

Possible Progressions:

- First time finishes count for 3 points.
- Add a neutral(s), so the attacking team is always numbers up (producing more scoring opportunities).
- Put field players on touch restrictions (e.g., 3 touch max).
- Put target players on a one touch restriction.

Activity #2: The 2 Zone Game

Time: Approximately 20 minutes.

Area: If you have a marked 18-yard box, use it and then mark out another one with cones to create a 36 x 44 yard (L x W) playing grid.

Activity: This game works best with 12 players (2 goalkeepers and 10 outfield players). If you have an assistant coach, have her work with the rest of the team on something else (e.g. a technical activity) and sub players in/out as appropriate, so all players on the team get to participate in both activities. Divide the players into 2 even (ability) teams with a goalkeeper in each goal. The balls should be divided evenly and placed in each goal for quick and easy retrieval by the goalkeeper. The rules are: Goalkeepers handle all restarts (I let the scoring team keep possession on goals, too); players can break the halfway line on offense, but not on defense; the goalkeeper must play the ball to a teammate in her own half. As it is 3v2 in the defending team's favor in each half, this set up encourages players to penetrate into the other half, as well as support. There are no offsides in this game. Also, mandate (to begin with) that all shots must come from within the attacking half. Players may not switch positions during the game (e.g. from the defensive half to the offensive half), but mandate rotation after each round. Play first team to a set number of goals (e.g. 5, 7, 9) and give the losing team a consequence. After the consequence, you can ask the guided discovery questions, while the players catch their breath.

Possible Progressions:

- Allow the goalkeeper to play direct to the forwards.
- Put all players on a touch restriction (e.g., 3 touch maximum).
- Mandate that all goals must be a first time finish.

Activity #3: The 3 Zone Game

Time: Approximately 20 minutes.

Area: If you have a marked 18-yard box, extend it sideways by 3-4 yards on each side, mark out another one with cones on the opposite side, and add a middle zone of about 18-22 yards to create 3 zones.

Activity: This game works best with 16 players (2 goalkeepers and 14 outfield players). Divide the players into 2 even (ability) teams with a goalkeeper in each goal. The balls should be divided evenly and placed in each goal for quick and easy retrieval by the goalkeeper. Similar to The 2 Zone Game, the rules are: Goalkeepers handle all restarts (I let the scoring team keep possession on goals, too); players can break a line on offense, but not on defense; the goalkeeper must play the ball to a teammate in her own half. As it is 3v2 in the defending team's favor in each defensive zone, this set up encourages players to penetrate into the next zone, as well as support. There are no offsides in this game. Mandate that a player can only pass the ball into the next zone (e.g. no ball is allowed to be played from the defensive zone to the attacking zone – players may dribble across the line, too). Also, mandate (to begin with) that all shots must come from within the attacking zone. Players may not switch positions during the game (e.g. from zone to zone), but mandate rotation after each round. Play first team to a set number of goals (e.g. 1-3) and give the losing team a consequence. After the consequence, you can ask the guided discovery questions, while the players catch their breath. I start players in their game positions in order to get them the necessary repetitions. It is also important to rotate them, though, so they see the bigger picture.

Possible Progressions:

- Remove the restriction that passes can only be played into the next zone.
- Put all players on a touch restriction (e.g. 3 touch maximum).

End of Practice Scrimmage: Get Over the Halfway Line!

Time: Approximately 30 minutes (or whatever is left of practice).

Area: As per the diagram, extend the 18-yard box out to the sidelines. This makes for a shorter, but wider playing area – perfect for working on crossing and finishing.

Activity: Use (or make) a halfway line and state that all players (except the goalkeeper) must be past it in order for a goal to count. This simple rule, more than anything, has the ability to teach players to get up and support the attack. Don't scream and shout at your players to "push up" over the halfway line. Just watch and listen. The first time that a team scores a goal and it doesn't count because one of the attacking team's defenders was in his own half, players on that team will start telling each other to "step" and "get up". It works like magic! Play even numbers and arrange teams in a formation that reflects your desired game day formation.

Progressions:

- If you catch a member of the opposing team in their attacking half, the goal counts double.
- Add a neutral(s), so the attacking team is always numbers up (producing more scoring opportunities).
- Put field players on touch restrictions (e.g., 3 touch max).

The Final Whistle

It is my hope that soccer coaches of all levels will find value in the concepts and activities that have been presented in this book. It is different from other coaching books insofar as it goes into detail about each session's purpose, set up, and the guided discovery questions that should be asked. While my philosophy is firmly rooted in a Game Based Soccer approach, the implementation of this is flexible. I view this book as a starting point for a discussion about how to create the best possible environment in which our soccer players can develop an attacking mindset, improve their skills, and - most of all - nurture a love for soccer.

To recap:
- Game-based soccer (GBS) training is the philosophy that all practice activities can and should be turned into a game.
- There should always be consequences for the losing person/team. "Consequences" should not be punishments and can be as simple as knowing that a particular team "lost" a particular game, picking up/resetting balls and cones, or a quick physical exertion (e.g., 5 knees to chest).
- Encourage the players to learn by doing.
- Allow players to make decisions and to deal with the consequences (in other words let them fail and let them figure out how to fix it. Only get involved if they try and can't fix it).
- Ask questions, rather than telling them what to do (this is tough!) because in the game, you can't control them like an avatar on an Xbox! Therefore, they need to think for themselves!
- Coach every player every day.
- Always end with a scrimmage!
- Don't be afraid to modify based on the needs of your own particular group of players.

Other Books from Bennion Kearny

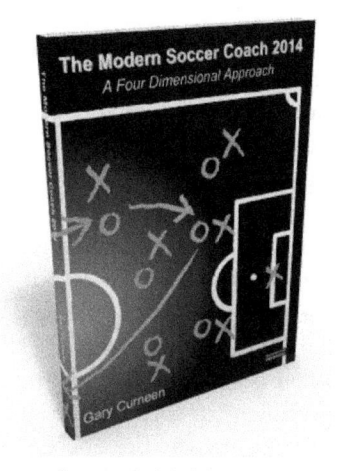

The Modern Soccer Coach by Gary Curneen

Aimed at Soccer coaches of all levels and with players of all ages and abilities The Modern Soccer Coach 2014 identifies the areas that must be targeted by coaches who want to maximize a team's potential – the Technical, Tactical, Physical, and Mental sides to the game. See how the game has changed and what areas determine success in the game today. Learn what sets coaches like Mourinho, Klopp, Rodgers, and Guardiola apart from the rest. Philosophies and training methods from the most forward thinking coaches in the game today are presented, along with guidelines on creating a modern environment for readers' teams. This book is not about old school methodologies – it is about creating a culture of excellence that gets the very best from players. Contains more than 30 illustrated exercises that focus on tactical, technical, mental, and physical elements of the game.

The Modern Soccer Coach: Pre-Season Training by Gary Curneen

When it comes to building successful soccer teams, pre-season is a critical time. It's the perfect time for the coach to create a team identity, set standards, develop effective training habits, and reinforce winning behaviors. Get it right and you can set the foundation required to catapult your team towards an excellent season. Get it wrong, however, and your season might never recover. This book looks at how pre-season has changed over the past 10 years, and offers ways for coaches to adapt their work and methods to deal with these changes accordingly. Pre-season is about much more than fitness testing, long-distance running, and grueling physical work. "The Modern Soccer Coach – Pre-Season Training" looks at new, innovative ways to engage players so that they want to train at the maximum every day, and push towards new limits for the new season ahead.

Soccer Tough: Simple Football Psychology Techniques to Improve Your Game by Dan Abrahams

"Take a minute to slip into the mind of one of the world's greatest soccer players and imagine a stadium around you. Picture a performance under the lights and mentally play the perfect game."

Technique, speed and tactical execution are crucial components of winning soccer, but it is mental toughness that marks out the very best players – the ability to play when pressure is highest, the opposition is strongest, and fear is greatest. Top players and coaches understand the importance of sport psychology in soccer but how do you actually train your mind to become the best player you can be? Soccer Tough demystifies this crucial side of the game and offers practical techniques that will enable soccer players of all abilities to actively develop focus, energy, and confidence. Soccer Tough will help banish the fear, mistakes, and mental limits that holds players back.

Coaching Psychological Skills in Youth Football: Developing The 5Cs by Chris Harwood and Richard Anderson

Successful footballers are typically those who are best able to: regulate their emotions, fix their attention, utilise effective interpersonal skills, and remain highly motivated and self-assured in the face of consistent challenges. These behaviours are the hallmark of mentally tough, emotionally intelligent players, and can be grouped under the 5Cs of: Commitment, Communication, Concentration, Control, and Confidence.

Written specifically for soccer coaches of all levels, Coaching Psychological Skills in Youth Football details each C in a methodical and practical manner with real-world exercises for training and matches. The book is relevant to soccer coaches working with 5-16 year old players, with individual techniques and practices marked for appropriate age groups.

Scientific Approaches to Goalkeeping in Football: A practical perspective on the most unique position in sport
by Andy Elleray

Do you coach goalkeepers and want to help them realise their fullest potential? Are you a goalkeeper looking to reach the top of your game? Then search no further and dive into this dedicated goalkeeping resource. Written by goalkeeping guru Andy Elleray this book offers a fresh and innovative approach to goalkeeping in football. With a particular emphasis on the development of young goalkeepers, it sheds light on training, player development, match performances, and player analysis. Utilising his own experiences Andy shows the reader various approaches, systems and exercises that will enable goalkeepers to train effectively and appropriately to bring out the very best in them.

The Modern Soccer Coach: Position-Specific Training by Gary Curneen

Aimed at football coaches of all levels, and players of all ages and abilities, The Modern Soccer Coach: Position-Specific Training seeks to identify, develop, and enhance the skills and functions of the modern soccer player whatever their position and role on the pitch.

This book offers unique insight into how to develop an elite program that can both improve players and win games. Filled with practical no-nonsense explanations, focused player drills, and more than 40 illustrated soccer templates, this book will help you – the modern coach - to create a coaching environment that will take your players to the next level.

The Footballer's Journey: real-world advice on becoming and remaining a professional footballer by Dean Caslake and Guy Branston

Many youngsters dream of becoming a professional footballer. But football is a highly competitive world where only a handful will succeed. Many aspiring soccer players don't know exactly what to expect, or what is required, to make the transition from the amateur world to the 'bright lights' in front of thousands of fans. The Footballer's Journey maps out the footballer's path with candid insight and no-nonsense advice. It examines the reality of becoming a footballer including the odds of 'making it', how academies really work, the importance of attitude and mindset, and even the value of having a backup plan if things don't quite work out.

Making The Ball Roll: A Complete Guide to Youth Football for the Aspiring Soccer Coach by Ray Power

Making the Ball Roll is the highly acclaimed, complete guide to coaching youth soccer.

This focused and easy-to-understand book details training practices and tactics, and goes on to show you how to help young players achieve peak performance through tactical preparation, communication, psychology, and age-specific considerations. Each chapter covers, in detail, a separate aspect of coaching to give you, the football coach, a broad understanding of youth soccer development. Each topic is brought to life by the stories of real coaches working with real players. Never before has such a comprehensive guide to coaching soccer been found in the one place. If you are a new coach, or just trying to improve your work with players - and looking to invest in your future - this is a must-read book!

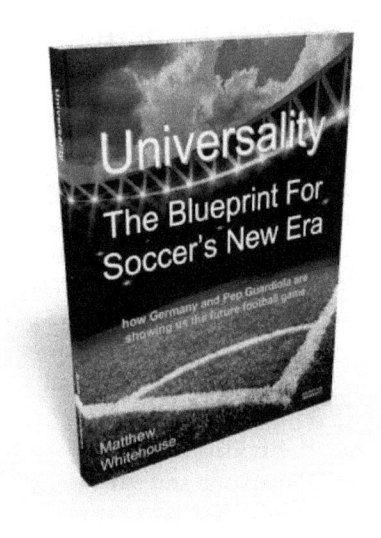

Universality | The Blueprint for Soccer's New Era: How Germany and Pep Guardiola are showing us the Future Football Game by Matthew Whitehouse

The game of soccer is constantly in flux; new ideas, philosophies and tactics mould the present and shape the future. In this book, Matthew Whitehouse – acclaimed author of The Way Forward: Solutions to England's Football Failings - looks in-depth at the past decade of the game, taking the reader on a journey into football's evolution. Examining the key changes that have occurred since the turn of the century, right up to the present, the book looks at the evolution of tactics, coaching, and position-specific play. They have led us to this moment: to the rise of universality. Universality | The Blueprint For Soccer's New Era is a voyage into football, as well as a lesson for coaches, players and fans who seek to know and anticipate where the game of the future is heading.

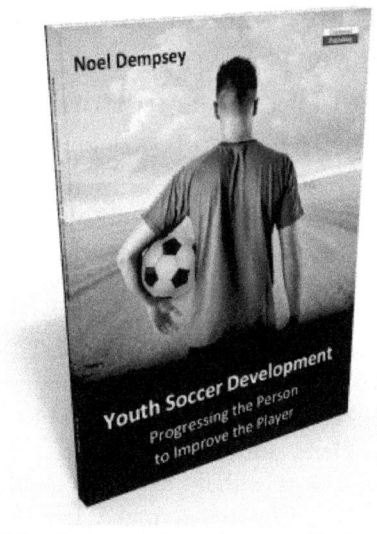

Youth Soccer Development: Progressing the Person to Improve the Player by Noel Dempsey

In "Youth Soccer Development", football coach Noel Dempsey examines where coaching has come from and where it is heading. Offering insights into how English football has developed, coaching methods, 'talent' in youngsters, and how a player's entire environment needs to be considered in coaching programmes - this book offers many touchpoints for coaches who want to advance their thinking and their coaching. Leaving specific onfield drills and exercises to other books, "Youth Soccer Development" digs deep into 'nature versus nature', players' core beliefs, confidence, motivation, and much more. Advocating that to improve the player, you must improve the person, Dempsey puts forward a case for coaches to be realistic with their players, ensure that they work positively across all facets of their lives - especially education - and to instil a mindset that leads to players being the best person they can be.

Developing the Modern Footballer through Futsal by Michael Skubala and Seth Burkett

Aimed at coaches of all levels and ages, Developing the Modern Footballer through Futsal is a concise and practical book that provides an easy-to-understand and comprehensive guide to the ways in which futsal can be used as a development tool for football. From defending and attacking to transitional play and goalkeeping, this book provides something for everyone and aims to get you up-and-running fast.

Over 50 detailed sessions are provided, with each one related to specific football scenarios and detailing how performance in these scenarios can be improved through futsal. From gegenpressing to innovative creative play under pressure, this book outlines how futsal can be used to develop a wide range of football-specific skills, giving your players the edge.

Deliberate Soccer Practice: 50 Passing & Possession Football Exercises to Improve Decision-Making by Ray Power

Aimed at football coaches of all levels, but with a particular emphasis on coaches who work with youth players, *50 Passing & Possession Football Exercises to Improve Decision-Making* is comprised of 20 Technical Practices and 30 Possession Practices. They are carefully designed to be adaptable to suit the needs of the players you work with; to challenge them and give them decisions to make. The sessions look to make soccer complex and realistically difficult – no passing in queues from one cone to the next with no interference. Crucially, the exercises offer a means to accelerate player development effectively and enjoyably.

Part of the *Deliberate Soccer Practice* series.

Other Recent Books from Bennion Kearny

Tipping The Balance: The Mental Skills Handbook For Athletes
by Dr Martin Turner & Dr Jamie Barker

The Bundesliga Blueprint: How Germany became the Home of Football by Lee Price

We publish a lot of books aimed at coaches, players, and football fans. Learn More about our Books at:

www.BennionKearny.com/Soccer

CPSIA information can be obtained
at www.ICGtesting.com
Printed in the USA
LVHW02s1209281017
554136LV00022B/299/P